INVINCIBLE

INVINCIBLE

MY JOURNEY FROM FAN TO NFL TEAM CAPTAIN

VINCE PAPALE

WITH CHAD MILLMAN

HYPERION

NEW YORK

Library of Congress Control Number: 2006927986

ISBN: 1-4013-0884-8 / 978-1-4013-0884-1

Hyperion books are available for special promotions and premiums.
For details contact Michael Rentas, Manager, Inventory and Premium Sales,
Hyperion, 77 West 66th Street, 12th floor, New York, New York 10023,
or call 212-456-0133.

FIRST PAPERBACK EDITION

10 9 8 7 6 5 4 3 2

To Mom and Dad for their spirit;

Janet, Gabriella, and Vincent for their inspiration;

George Corner for his guidance;

Dick Vermeil for the opportunity;

and Jefferson Hospital for a second chance!

ACKNOWLEDGMENTS

AM INDEBTED not only to the people who shaped my life, but to those who helped me put it on the page, including:

My wife, Janet, our daughter, Gabriella, and our son, Vincent, who bring me more joy than a thousand Sundays at the Vet ever could.

George Corner, Marty Stern, and Dick Vermeil, my coaches for life.

The students and teachers at Interboro High School, who taught me how to persevere.

Jim Gallagher, Jim Murray, and Denny Franks at the Eagles, who helped keep my dreams alive.

Pete DiStefano at NFL Films, who remembered my story and brought it back to life. Bruce Casella for keeping it alive.

The writers who covered the Eagles for the *Daily News*, the

Bulletin, the *Inquirer*, and the *Delaware County Daily Times*, whose old articles helped me remember countless details.

Pro Football Hall of Fame sportswriter Ray Didinger, who played against me when we were boys, covered me as a pro and co-authored, with Robert Lyons, the definitive Eagles reference book, *The Eagles Encyclopedia*, which was invaluable while working on this project.

The Eagles PR staff—Derek Boyko, Rich Burg, Bob Lange, and Jake Greenbaum—for digging through the files and helping me fill in game details.

My attorney Vincent Carissimi, for guiding me through the process, literary agent Richard Abate at ICM, who put the project together, and my editor at Hyperion, Zareen Jaffery, whose deft touch made this a better book.

INVINCIBLE

ONE

WE CALLED ourselves the project boys, the kids of cinder-block city. Me and Albert Friel and Frankie Falcone and Billy Sides and Bobby Joe Hazel, who was our local celebrity because his uncle Del Ennis was a Phillies outfielder and his mom was real foxy. We were poor, and weren't ever made to believe we were anything but, and we thought we were tough, or at least we fought like we were. Because when you're from the project all you know is that you're not as good as the kids who aren't. And we spent our lives trying to convince ourselves that wasn't true.

Our housing project, the Glendale Heights Ownership Association, was built during the Second World War on an old golf course in Glenolden, Pennsylvania. My family moved there in 1945, the year before I was born. The project was in Delaware County, the suburbs of Philadelphia, connected to the city by a factory-lined road called the Industrial Highway. But Philly might as well have been as far away as California to us. The people there seemed like aliens. My friends and I shared urban myths about the hoods in leather jackets who hung around fires built in tin cans singing doo-wop songs.

My parents, Francis and Almira, grew up in Delaware County. My father started working as a burner cutting sheet metal at the Westinghouse factory on Industrial in 1946, when he was twenty-seven years old. Before that he had been building houses. We lived on Andrews Avenue in a house barely big enough to hold a dining room table. A phone hung next to the closet, and behind those doors was the only place you could get any privacy. My bedroom was so long and thin we weren't able to fit a bed in there and close the door. And from my window I could hear the whistle of the Baltimore & Ohio Railroad. My parents had been living in an old stucco farmhouse on my grandfather's farm that he had converted into an apartment. My grandfather had nine kids and all of them, after they were first married, lived in that apartment. When my parents moved to this home in the project, the first that they owned together, it was supposed to be a step up in life. My dad built a patio, planted a garden in front of that, put up a green awning, kept our used Pontiac with the junk-yard parts parked in a space out front, and stashed a loaded .22 in his room. That was to shoot the rats. All the homes in the project were small and cheap. To us, any place where you couldn't hear the neighbors snoring would have been an improvement. One summer in the early 1950s a group of college kids who thought they were doing a community service for those of us less fortunate painted all the houses in the neighborhood in pastel colors. By the end of the winter, the bright pinks and blues and yellows had begun to peel and blister, making every house look like a cracked Easter egg. The next spring, the housing association covered the houses in aluminum siding.

Whatever my father thought he was getting when he moved us into the project, it didn't stay that way for long.

Most of the dads I knew from the project were factory shift workers, all dressed in blue work shirts and blue work pants, carrying metal lunch pails and packs of Pall Malls. They had to finish their morning coffee and be out of the house by 7:30 to make the 8 A.M. whistle. You could see the cars pulling out from in front of their houses as though their departures had all been synchronized, like dominoes falling down one after the other. By the time they finally pulled onto Lincoln Highway there were never any accidents because no one ever went anywhere. My dad was a member of the United Electrical Workers Union, and he'd go on strike anytime one of his fellow members was sent home, whether it was justified or not. They'd walk out if a line worker who got drunk during lunch was told to go sleep it off for the rest of the afternoon. It seemed as if they were constantly striking. And every time they did it hit us hard. It always felt like we would never recover. There were close to thirty guys who worked at Westinghouse that lived in the project. I remember calls from the shop steward to my mom, telling her my dad was on his way home and everyone from the project was going to huddle together and figure out what to do next. Sometimes my dad would pick up work as a mechanic. Other times he'd drive a trash truck around West Philly. And occasionally he'd walk the picket line. It seemed as if there was always something dangerous going on there, men being beaten, cars being flipped over and torched.

My father wasn't a big man, but my aunts, uncles, cousins, and his friends called him Kingie, because he always won when they played king of the hill. Nobody messed with him. He had grown up on a fourteen-acre farm where the town used to dump all the garbage, so the pigs his father owned could forage through it and have something to eat. My grandfather Vincenzo had bowlegs and hairy ears and hairy nostrils. He came to the United States from Italy with his father in 1899, when he was seven years old. The two of them settled on a farm in Delaware County and then sent for his mom and five younger brothers and sisters. Vincenzo Papale had a wonderful singing voice and he and all his brothers used to play instruments like the viola or the violin and sing together on Sunday afternoons.

My grandfather believed the oldest children were to sacrifice for the youngest, which is why he and his nearest brother in age worked the farms and pushed their younger siblings to go to school. His youngest brother, Tony, would become a lawyer and, eventually, the dean of Loyola University in New Orleans. Vincenzo Papale also subscribed to the parenting philosophy that children were to be seen and not heard. My dad was the second oldest of the nine Papale kids, and he and the oldest, his brother Gus, had to quit school in eighth grade to work on the farm. This was during the Depression and my grandfather needed to supplement what he made working the assembly line at a local Ford factory by selling beets, corn, and tomatoes at local markets. He even sang around town with his hat in his hand. He developed a work ethic that would last for the rest of his life. For thirty years he worked at that Ford plant, changing jobs as he got older from assembly line worker to spray painter to forklift operator. He'd work from seven in the morning until three in the afternoon, then come home and spend three hours tilling the farm. When he was done he'd take what he had picked and sell it in the local markets. And what he didn't sell he canned. All his children had fresh spaghetti sauce year round because of all the tomatoes he produced. But the sting of the Depression would never leave him.

Like so many people during those lean years, the times made him hard and angry. Years later my aunt Suzanne, who was actually born three years after me, when my grandfather was fifty-eight, would say, "Daddy, tell me about the Depression." My grandfather would respond, "Well, there were men with one child jumping off bridges. And I had eight."

He'd often take it out on his oldest boys, not just in work, but also in anger or, worse, indifference. One afternoon my dad was cleaning the family outhouse and got some lye in his eye. He was screaming, stumbling around the farm looking for help from anyone who could hose down his eye. When his father found him he washed out the lye. And then told him to get back outside to finish working. My father's eye was so badly damaged he became legally blind.

Given the way he grew up, it's no surprise my father sometimes acted as though my mother and sister and I were burdens. He didn't know any better. The most emotional I ever saw him get was after our cat, Mittens, killed his parakeet, Pretty Boy. He loved that bird. It used to perch itself on the edge of his newspaper and it looked like the two of them were reading it together. I think he talked to Pretty Boy more than he talked to me. At times it seemed he definitely loved that parakeet more than he loved my mom. When it died he cried, and I remember saying to myself, Come on Dad, you should have known better than to leave the cage open with Mittens around. Mittens disappeared the next day.

My father never hit us, but it wasn't a house where we heard the words "I love you" very often. He wasn't the type of person who would allow you to get close to him. I never disliked him or resented him. I just wanted to please him. There were times—like when we picked him up from the factory—when I thought he was as cool as can be. He'd come strolling out, his dark hair parted neatly down the middle and a cigarette hanging from his mouth. When he'd get in the car he wouldn't say a word. At home he'd have his dinner, sit in his reclining chair, have a beer, and fall asleep. There was no conversation, no interaction whatsoever. Albert Friel's dad was quiet like mine. So were Bobby Herkertt's and Bobby Joe Hazel's. The men my friends and I grew up knowing were all so exhausted, so consumed with working and trying to make

ends meet, no father stood out from any other. We barely
talked to them, they barely talked to us, and nobody thought
there was anything wrong with that.

As kids we were more interested in the games we played.
Our house was the last one before the small park that split the
project in the middle. It was once the ninth fairway of the
golf course the project was built on. That's where the kids of
cinder-block city learned to compete. And time stood still
when we did. It didn't matter if it was a real game or one we
made up. We'd play Wiffle ball, acting out games between
every team in the National League—all the Phillies' rivals—
plus the Yankees. We'd go through the lineups and bat left-
handed or right-handed, depending on which player we were
pretending to be. We played basketball on the court that was
built just beyond my backyard. If we were lucky we could
find a football, which we'd play with until the edges were
worn down to the cotton. We played capture using a big
maple tree in my backyard as home base. We played kick the
can and roller derby in the street in front of all of our houses.
And we made up a game called monkeyball, in which we
tried to hit one another with huge fruit that fell from the
trees. The Jenkins brothers and the Sides brothers were the
bad guys and me and Albert and Bobby Joe were the good
guys. We were always outside our houses because they were so
tiny. And how well you played sports—your ability to catch,
throw, run, or jump—meant everything to us. It was our
caste system. And I was the smallest.

But I was faster than anyone.

* * *

I COULD NEVER be caught in capture, never get tackled in football, and never get hit with fruit in monkeyball. On the summer holidays, or just about any day when the adults weren't working, we'd have races through the old ninth fairway. All the dads would sit in their lawn chairs, pop open a Schlitz, which was just ninety-nine cents for a six-pack, and make bets on the kids. I always went off at 1–5. I was the Seabiscuit of the neighborhood always running in bare feet. When the dads would win a buck, they'd kick back a quarter to me. Except on the Fourth of July, when I'd get three bucks for winning a race. I'd come home with ten dollars in my pocket.

The speed made me fearless and gave me a confidence I lacked in just about everything else I did. I was a little kid. When I was fourteen I was still shorter than five feet and weighed no more than a hundred pounds. I didn't get much attention at home and I honestly didn't want to be noticed anywhere else. I wasn't the kid who raised his hand in class or felt comfortable talking to girls, especially because of my bad acne. But when I played anything, I forgot about that. I just ran and then I felt proud. I knew trouble couldn't catch me, no matter what I did. I would swing from the tallest tree or climb the highest roof (usually to sneak peeks of Bobby Joe's mom sunbathing in a bikini in her front yard). Glenolden Park was just a mile from the project. It looked like a big grass bowl, with a field and a creek—we called it a "crick"—at the bottom and steep hills on all sides. In the summer, that's where the project kids went to free summer camp. But in the winter, we took our Flexible Flyers and tried to get enough speed going down the hill to skid across the bridge that covered the water. That crick ran from Glenolden Park all the way down to the project. It was surrounded by tall thickets of grass and was filled with water that came up to our waists. When it stormed we'd find old pieces of wood and surf the crick, floating from the project to the park. I also liked to take bamboo poles that had been wrapped inside new rugs, get a running start toward the crick, plant the pole in the deepest part of the water, and vault myself across. When I was seven I jumped off the Hazels' chicken coop and broke my arm. As soon as I got the cast off I tried pole-vaulting the creek. Of course I fell, landed on a nail, and shattered the arm again.

When I was nine years old my guys and I had to switch schools, leaving the smaller MacDade School, which was mainly for kids from the project, for the Logan Avenue School, which was on the more affluent side of town. It was the first time any of the boys from the project interacted on a daily basis with kids who weren't as poor as we were. To get to school we walked through a small tunnel, no wider or longer than a single car, along one of the sides of Glenolden Park, which was the line of demarcation between rich and poor. The homes on that side of the tunnel were beautiful old Victorians. And every time we walked through it we got anxious, as if we were going to be stopped and told to turn around. Even in school, I was so small I was afraid to look any of the kids I didn't know in the eye. I wanted to be invisible.

At least until we had our field day early in the fall. It was a real chamber of commerce day. All of the classes—third, fourth, fifth, and sixth—were gathered around the playground. We were playing kickball and the ball had to come in on three bounces, each one weaker, like a fading pulse. As the kicker you wanted to get it just as it hit the ground that third time. And I nailed it, catching the red rubber ball on the top of my right foot, sending it clear over the fence. I ran around the bases in a blur, not hearing the crowd screaming until I crossed home plate. It was the first time anyone my age had ever cheered for me. The next day in school, kids I didn't even know greeted me with a "Hey, Vinny." And I wasn't scared anymore.

TWO

"VINCIE, VINCIE." I could hear my mom screaming my name from our house, begging me to come home. I would be down by the crick playing and her voice would crack from our window, scaring my friends and me until we realized who it was.

"Vincie, Vincie." The first couple of times I heard her I was so frightened I raced home. But the more it happened, the less concerned I became. When I'd get home, she'd be upset because a dresser drawer had been left open half an inch and she needed me to close it. I always did, and then I went back out to play. My mom was slowly succumbing to mental illness, and there was nothing I could do to stop it.

My mom had always been the parent who was the most athletic, the one whom I looked to play with after school if no one else was around. She was the fourth of eight kids, and the first girl, which meant she was always competing to keep up with her three older brothers. In 1937 she had been a shortstop for the St. Raphael Bobbies—a barnstorming women's baseball team that traveled up and down the East Coast. She was just five-four, but her nickname was Big Al. In one letter from her coach he said she earned the nickname because she was always making big plays. In our house, there was a picture of her posing in her uniform. She's got a grin full of straight white teeth, jet-black hair circling her face, and she is looking up at her outstretched arm, at the end of which is a glove cradling a ball. The whole family—my cousins, aunts, uncles, and grandparents on my mother's side—used to visit Lake Kaolin in Paoli, where my mom's father, Sidney Sage, had a cabin. There was a diving board on the lake and I would watch her do the most perfect swan dives. She was naturally fluid and graceful; nothing she did physically seemed to take any effort. In the housing project, we'd play catch—she still had her old mitt—and run races in the middle of Andrews Avenue. She had a wonderful stride, and I'd try to match her all the way down the block.

My parents were married in 1940, a year after my uncle Gus accidentally set them up. Both my dad and Gus worked at a gas station across the street from my mom's house. She often came in to fill up her car and Uncle Gus and she became friends. One day they were supposed to spend the afternoon together, but when my mom arrived, Gus was too busy and told my dad to take her out. He did. And a year later they were married.

My mom came from a comfortable family—her father was

an electrician for the Pennsylvania Railroad—and they lived in an airy three-story house on a property surrounded by forsythias and hydrangeas. We used to sit for hours in rocking chairs on the front porch. They had a four-car garage that was filled with Fords, and I used to love going in there to smell the cold, pressed-dirt floor. After she married my dad, those material comforts would be gone for good. But, at least early on in their marriage, they seemed happy. They'd bowl often. At weddings they were the first ones on the dance floor. On Saturday nights my mom and dad shared highballs with friends and relatives in our living room and then went out to listen to Bill Haley and His Comets and dance the jitterbug. My mom never complained that her kids usually drank powdered milk and water or that standard fare had become potato-salad sandwiches.

But when I was seven years old her demeanor changed. She began waking up in the middle of the night and pacing our hallway, complaining of an incessant ringing in her head. She would say it sounded like a telephone that she couldn't ever answer. Some nights she would hold a radio to her ear and turn it up as loud as it would go, trying to drown out the noise. My dad, my sister, and I didn't understand what was happening, and the tension in the house became unbearable. My mom was functional—she still had dinner on the table for my father by 4:30—but uncomfortable and unable to explain why. Suddenly my parents were fighting all the time, with my dad not understanding what was happening to his wife and my mom receding into her head more and more.

Then, one afternoon in the summer of 1955, when I was nine years old, we were in our Pontiac headed for a vacation. My father saved money all year so the four of us could take a week off before school started and spend it on the Jersey shore. Mom and Dad were in the middle of a fierce argument, their voices filling the car with rage. Dad pulled the car to a stop thanks to a traffic jam in the middle of the Penrose Avenue Bridge, which connected Penrose Avenue to the Industrial Highway and ran over the Schuylkill River. It was packed with cars, all of them going toward the shore for one last summer getaway. My mother may have been getting sick, but she never backed down from a fight. In fact, the worse she became, the fewer inhibitions she showed. She laid into my dad as harshly as he laid into her. But in the car that day, sitting in traffic on the bridge, she abruptly stopped yelling. Instead of responding to what my father was shouting about, she looked at him and said, "I'm going to jump." She said it as calmly as if she were telling us she was going to the market. Then she got out of the car, walked over to the edge of the bridge's railing, and leaned over, staring into the bottom of the Schuylkill.

I couldn't believe what I was seeing. But the looks on the faces of the people in the cars behind us told me that what was happening was real. My father was two steps behind my mom as soon as she got out of the car. To this day I don't know if she was really going to jump, but that moment when she leaned over the railing and stared into the water was all the hesitation my father needed to grab her by the waist and pull her back. He walked her to the car, waited for the traffic to clear, and just kept going for the shore. Thank God we did that. While the next couple hours in the car were tense and quiet, much worse than when my parents fought, going home to our cookie-cutter house would have been unbearable. I desperately needed that escape. Once we arrived at the beach my sister and I played with our cousins and we all went about our lives. We never discussed what had happened. But to this day I'm still petrified to drive over bridges.

Over the next several years my mom just faded in and out mentally and emotionally. Even in photographs she looks vacant and distant. Her body angles away from everyone else in the picture. Her weight fluctuated and she began dyeing her hair garish colors. Our house, which she once kept immaculate, was in disarray. We had always been poor, but I never felt ashamed or that anyone else in the project was any better off than we were. That was no longer true and I was embarrassed to have my friends over. When I was ten years old I began washing my pants and getting up early to iron my clothes. This was how I tried to help her. I didn't know what else to do.

AFTER THAT SUMMER, it would be hard to call what my parents had a marriage. They never divorced and my dad never left us. But one night he threatened to walk out. My sister and I clung to his legs and begged him to stay. But the little passion they shared early on was burned off by her illness and my dad's frustration—with her, with his job, and, as far as I knew, with me.

At around the same time that my mom became sick I started playing organized sports. My dad would never miss a game, but he never cheered. He'd just sit in the stands or on the sideline, usually alone. I'd look at him and his expression wouldn't change. But he'd always have something to say when the game was over. I played Pee Wee football in Glenolden Park and during one game our coaches, two med students named Dave and Steve Bosacco, called a reverse for me deep at our end of the field. I took the handoff, raced toward the sideline, cut back toward the middle, and sprinted toward the end zone. I was so small my pads were flopping back and forth on my shoulders and riding up into my chin. Once I scored I was so tired I fell face-first into the end zone. Yet, after the game, my father didn't congratulate me for scoring. He said to me, "Don't ever fall in the end zone again." He thought I was showing up the other team.

When he joined a group of other fathers and created the Glendale Boys Club baseball team—and made me quit Wiffle ball because he thought it would ruin my timing—I figured it was so he could find more ways to criticize me. Same when he decided to co-coach my under-100-pound football team. Otherwise why would he bother? In one game we played against a team called the Prospect Termites at Witmer Field. They had a kid my age named Mike Paynter who had the biggest thighs that I had ever seen. I bent down to tackle him and the next thing I knew I was seeing stars. I was just out cold. I didn't wake up until I was in the hospital with a concussion. But even that didn't stem the flow of criticism. Now my dad was finally talking to me at dinner; he talked real slowly and deliberately, but I hated it because all he did was critique my play.

My father was a frustrated jock. He was cheated, really, out of ever finding out how good he could have been because of when he quit school. He was an avid golfer, bowler, and loved doing anything physical outside. But what he loved most was playing semi-pro football. He played for a team in a town called Marcus Hook, which made the Glenolden project look upscale. It was a tough, working-class town along the Delaware River on the New Jersey and Pennsylvania border with a skyline full of smokestacks and dirty gray clouds that billowed high into the sky. They were semi-pro not because someone sponsored every team and paid the players, but because the players passed a hat around to everyone watching and asked them to contribute.

My father played running back and he was fast, not just running end zone to end zone, but between tacklers who were doing more than trying to take him down—they wanted to knock him out. These were guys who didn't go to college, a lot of them probably didn't even finish high school. They were just coming back from the war. The emotions and reasons for playing in those Sunday afternoon games were as varied as the types of rocks that littered the field. Some guys were trying to prove something to themselves, others wanted to prove their worth to somebody else. And some guys just wanted to crack somebody's head, whether they were sick of their factory jobs or trying to fit back into society after a couple years in battle.

They wore leather helmets with no face masks, shoulder pads that were no thicker than the Sunday newspaper, and hip pads made of beaten down cotton that were sewn into their pants.

The games were so tough—every player was on edge and ready to fight—that no one was immune. During one game while my mom and dad were still courting each other, my uncle Joe and my dad got into an argument about a call. It escalated quickly and ended even faster, after my dad popped Joe in the mouth and knocked out a tooth. My parents stopped dating for a while after that.

Sports meant everything to my dad. Whether he was playing or just watching, they were a release for him in a way his family could never be. From the time he was thirteen years old his life had been about work and responsibility, about sacrificing himself to take care of someone else through hard, monotonous labor. Sports were just about pleasure. On Friday nights he'd sit back in his recliner, pop open a beer, and watch local legends like Joey Giardello on the Friday night fights. It was one of the few times we could sit together and have silence indicate joy, not tension. We shared the experience. Happily. He let me take a sip of his beer and we made cheese and cracker sandwiches.

But the Philadelphia Eagles were his true love. On Sunday mornings he'd walk a mile to attend Our Lady of Fatima Church by himself (my mom was a Protestant and refused to raise my sister and me Catholic, yet another source of tension between my parents). When he came home he'd wheel the television over to the dining room table and make us all eat a traditional Italian lunch while watching the Eagles play. I don't know that my mom and my sister cared all that much who won or lost. But loving the Eagles became something else my dad and I had in common. No one said a word, of course. Not even during commercials. We were too locked in on the game. Or we were stuffing ourselves with the spaghetti and meatballs and fresh sauce my mom had somehow pulled herself together long enough to make. The Eagles became a part of the fabric of our family, which made us no different from nearly every other family in and around Philadelphia.

WHEN BERT BELL and other investors bought the NFL's Philly franchise in 1933 for $2,500, he changed the name of the team from the Frankford Yellow Jackets to the Philadelphia Eagles, after the symbol President Franklin Roosevelt chose for the National Recovery Act. But it would be years before Bell's team learned to fly. In five seasons as coach, owner, PR man, trainer, and just about every other job in the organization, Bell had led his team to just ten wins. Bell could have been doing anything other than running a team that was drowning in debt yearly. He came from a wealthy Main Line Philadelphia family that owned the Ritz and St. James hotels in Philadelphia and was a World War I war hero. His father was the state's attorney general. His brother would do the same job and even serve as governor. Meanwhile, Bell graduated from Penn and became a football coach, serving his alma mater and then Temple before buying the Eagles. He was a football man to the core.

While Bell's teams weren't very good, his fellow owners could see how passionate he was for the game. Which is why, in 1946, he was asked to become the NFL's commissioner. It meant giving up the Eagles, but he would define the modern NFL. He supported the players' union and imposed revenue sharing so rich teams and poor teams benefited from increasingly valuable TV contracts. He created the draft so big-time teams like Chicago and New York couldn't outspend small teams like Green Bay on the best college players. He personally devised the league schedule every year at his kitchen table so the great match-ups happened throughout the season. He made himself easily available to the press so the league always had good PR. And, in 1956, he came up with the rule that perhaps saved the league: sudden-death overtime. Even through the 1950s professional football was a distant second to the college game. But in late December 1958 the Baltimore Colts and the New York Giants played the NFL Championship game at Yankee Stadium. The game was tied at the end of regulation and, with millions of people watching, went into sudden-death overtime. In a contest still called "The Greatest Game Ever Played," the Colts' running back Alan Ameche scored the game-winning touchdown from the one-yard line. It wasn't long before pro football passed not just college football but baseball as America's pastime.

Bell became the league's commissioner at the same time the Eagles were becoming the team Philly fans loved most. After years of futility, they finished above .500 for the first time in 1943 and stayed above it for the next six seasons. In 1947 they finished in first place in their division for the first time in their history. In 1948 they won the NFL title. Fans showed up in a snowstorm that was so bad the Eagles' star running back, Steve Van Buren, woke up the day of the championship game, was sure it would be cancelled, and rolled over and went back to sleep. The Eagles won the title again in 1949. It takes just one championship and the generation of sports fans that came before and the generation that come after are hooked. Two championships and no son born in the city for fifty years will know anything other than the glory of those seasons. And no one ever completely gives up on their first love. Bert Bell certainly didn't.

In mid-October 1959, Bell was watching the Eagles play the Steelers at Franklin Field, the football stadium on Penn's campus, where he had played and coached and which his family once owned. The game was close and, in the final two minutes, Eagles wide receiver Tommy McDonald scored a touchdown. It was the last play Bell would ever see. He died of a heart attack seconds after McDonald scored. Years later his family would find out that that week he had planned to step down as commissioner and buy back his beloved Eagles.

THERE WERE SOME days when I felt I could completely relate to what Bell must have been feeling the day he died. Because after their back-to-back titles at the end of the forties, the Eagles took a dive in the mid-to-late fifties, winning just thirteen games between 1955 and 1958. The only things the fans looked forward to were the draft picks the Eagles would make in the spring. And in 1957, they chose Tommy McDonald, who had just won the Maxwell Award naming him the best player in college football. Of course, his intro to Philly was as abysmal as the team's play. After picking up the Maxwell Award he went for a walk through town to learn about his new city. Unfortunately for McDonald, he bore a striking resemblance to a serial burglar known as the Kissing Bandit that was terrorizing the city. When McDonald walked into a shop the woman behind the counter screamed, and two of Philly's finest came rushing through the door. They threw McDonald against the wall and only after he convinced them to call the Eagles front office did they let him go.

McDonald was my hero. Just five-nine, 176 pounds, he was a man among giants on the field. But he was rarely hurt, because no one could catch him. (And if they did hurt him, it still didn't stop him. In 1959 he broke his jaw in the season opener, had it wired shut during the week, and played the next weekend.) He had blue eyes and blond hair, and had been an All-American at Oklahoma, where his team didn't lose a game in the three seasons he played there. Yet, because of his size, he wasn't picked until the third round of the draft. Even the Eagles tried him at two other positions they thought someone of his stature would be more suited for before finally letting him line up as a receiver. He was tough, fast, fearless, and cocky. Everything I wanted to be. Vince Lombardi once said of him, "If I had eleven Tommy McDonalds I would win a championship every year." I couldn't wait to read everything about him, hear everything about him, and watch everything about him on TV. Over five seasons, from 1958 to 1962, he averaged nearly one touchdown a game, scoring once every six catches. Almost every time he caught the ball, the Eagles gained nearly twenty yards. After games I would go into the backyard and pretend I was Tommy McDonald, catching touchdowns. Or I used to lie on the floor in the living room, throw a football into the air, try to roll all the way over, and then catch it before it hit the ground. Tommy McDonald wore Riddell cleats, so I had to wear Riddell cleats. He wore a helmet without a face mask, so I wanted to wear a helmet without a face mask. He sandpapered his fingers before games because he said it made his fingertips more sensitive, so I wanted to do that, too. I liked the way he talked and walked and ran. I liked his persona and the way he caught the ball. I used to fantasize about meeting Tommy McDonald.

My whole life revolved around the Eagles. I couldn't digest enough about them. In 1960, when I was fourteen, the Eagles finally made it back to the NFL title game against the Green Bay Packers. It was the day after Christmas, and I was sitting in my room, listening to the game being broadcast on the radio from Franklin Field and going ballistic. Norm Van Brocklin was the quarterback. He was in the last season of his Hall of Fame career and played as though his only intention was to go out a winner. McDonald didn't let him down, catching thirty-nine passes that season, thirteen of them for touchdowns.

Early in the championship game the Packers were ahead 6–0 when Van Brocklin lofted a thirty-five-yard pass to McDonald, who caught it for a touchdown, giving the Eagles a 7–6 lead. For the next two quarters I had my ear practically glued to my radio as both teams went back and forth, with only the Eagles managing a second-quarter field goal to go up 10–6. Then, less than two minutes into the fourth quarter, the Packers drove the ball nearly the length of the field to go ahead 13–10. But, on the Packers' kickoff, an Eagle rookie named Ted Dean, who had grown up outside Philly, returned the ball fifty-eight yards to the Packers' forty. Moments later he ran a sweep around left end to give the Eagles a 17–13 lead with a little less than ten minutes remaining in the game.

But these were Vince Lombardi's Packers, with Bart Starr and Max McGee and Paul Hornung and Jim Taylor. There was still a lot of time left for them to score another touchdown. Late in the game, before I had even finished running through the list of their superstars in my head, the Packers had marched from their own thirty-five-yard line down to the Eagles' twenty-two.

With less than a minute left, Taylor caught a pass from Starr and began racing for the end zone, when Eagles linebacker Chuck Bednarik slammed him to the turf. I had seen these guys play so often on TV and heard their names called too many times on the radio not to know that Bednarik was loving the fact that the end of the game was in his hands.

Bednarik was in his twelfth year in the league, all twelve of which had been spent playing both center and linebacker. He was the last of the sixty-minute men, that breed of players who never took off a down. He had been a star at Penn and was the Eagles' top pick in 1949, the last time they won the NFL title. He came back during the 1960 season only because he was promised he'd just have to play center. But when one of the Eagles' starting linebackers was injured early in the year, he had no choice. He was as nasty and ruthless and savvy on the field as he was tireless, which is how he could get away with bear-hugging Jim Taylor and letting the clock run out. He refused to let go. And the game ended like that, with the Packers stalled at the Eagles' nine-yard line and my team as the NFL champs.

This was a rough Christmas for us. My mom was in a particularly bad state. We didn't have many presents under the tree. The Eagles were my escape from it all. When they were winning I didn't think about being ashamed because of my mother or wonder what my father was going to criticize next. The only thing that mattered was that the Eagles had won, that Tommy McDonald had scored a touchdown, and that I could see myself on the field celebrating with him.

THREE

WALT BUECHELE was the science teacher at Interboro Junior High School. But he was also the seventh-grade track coach, and when school started each fall, he'd spend most of recess on the field keeping an eye out for the fastest kids. In 1958, I was the fastest kid on the playground. And by the end of my first week at school, Buechele had me on his track team. He had a blond, bushy flattop that was so fine it looked like it would tickle your hand if you rubbed the top of it. He was soft spoken and reserved and had a full-wattage smile that made all his kids feel at ease. I ran the sprints and the 60-, 80-, and 100-yard hurdles and the 4×100 relays. But that year, running track wasn't about how well our team performed or what races I won individually. Seventh-grade track was something to do after school. It taught us how to be a part of a team. And, for an undersized kid with problems at home, it was a good way to release anger and energy and express myself in ways I never could otherwise.

But, in eighth and ninth grade, track became a serious sport where competition was fierce and the score was kept— and that was just during practice. This was mainly because of the eighth-grade coach, Marty Stern. An Air Force vet who was the Air Force's quarter-mile champ, he was the Rolls-Royce of track coaches. He graduated from West Chester State Teachers College in 1959 after earning letters in track, cross-country, and wrestling. He was just five-foot-four, but, like the diminutive Tommy McDonald, that's partially what I liked about him. He was small, powerful, commanding, and, most of all, intense. He would scream and curse, throw batons and shoes. After college he ran with some local track clubs and stayed in great shape, so every practice he'd train right beside us. He could run like the wind. Years later he would become the head track coach at Villanova University and lead the women's team to five straight NCAA cross-country titles. And he worked us as if we were preparing for the Penn Relays, not an after-school meet at Sharon Hill Junior High down the road.

We didn't even have our own track. Instead we had to run around Witmer Field, which is where Mike Paynter had knocked me out. That's where Marty taught me how to run. He noticed that I was clenching my fists when I ran, which forced me to lock up my forearms and biceps and shoulders, and then my arms would swing across the front of my body, not pump along the sides. So he taught me how to relax my hands. He had us practice just touching our thumbs and forefingers together on each hand. He had us think of our arms as the pistons on a locomotive, working completely in sync, going forward and back. Relaxing us while we ran, letting our legs do the work of carrying us while the rest of our bodies just helped our legs, became his sole focus for a few weeks, to the point where he had us work on relaxing our jaws as we ran by mumbling slack-jawed. We called it the blabber drill.

This was the first time I experienced coaching other than hearing from one of our dads or the guys who were helping out with Boys Club baseball or Pee Wee football. Marty cared about this in a way that made us feel important, as though it were his life's work to help a bunch of eleven-, twelve-, and thirteen-year-olds get faster. At one meet an official tried to disqualify our relay team for a bad exchange and Marty went nuts. He was on the track yelling, his face turning red. We all stared at him and felt, well, proud. He cared about winning, about us winning, as much as we did. I had never had an advocate like that before.

My speed and effort got me noticed. In eighth-grade phys-ed class, among a group of twenty boys, I stood out. The gym teacher, George Corner, happened to be the eighth-grade basketball coach as well, and he didn't care that I was barely four-eleven. He judged me for my heart and enthusiasm and he figured I'd at least wear opponents out, so he put me on the team. I was shy and maybe he saw that in me, because he tried to draw me out. He taught us how to wear jockstraps and that you should change your socks after gym class. During lunch he'd shoot hoops with me. Or he'd sneak up behind me and pinch my shoulder and playfully scream, "What's that muscle, what's that muscle?" He wouldn't let go until I could stop laughing long enough to say, "Trapezius." After a while that wasn't good enough and he'd make me spell it out. He showered me with attention and, being starved for it at home, I just wanted to please him. He was consistent, disciplined, and, in my eyes, perfect—everything I wanted for a father. He became a surrogate for me, living an idyllic life that I dreamed about. He was handsome, just twenty-two years old, had a beautiful wife, and was respected at school. Even the way he wrote was precise.

And maybe he saw a little bit of himself in me. George was from my area and his dad had raised him. His mom was a schizophrenic who spent her adult life in state hospitals. And then the same thing happened to his sister. Growing up he felt responsible for both of them, guilty that he wasn't in their place and afraid that one day he might be. When he graduated from State Teachers College at Lock Haven he almost took a job at a very small school on the Pennsylvania–New Jersey border because it was near the mental facility his sister was in. Only after her doctor dressed him down for living his life worrying about her, instead of for himself, did he move back home and get a job at his alma mater, Interboro.

George knew things weren't right for me at home. Everyone in town knew it. My parents came to all my eighth-grade basketball games and they were just about the oddest couple you can imagine sitting in the stands. My father, as usual, watched intently and said nothing. But my mom could not control herself. Her disease had completely taken hold of her. She'd yell at the refs incessantly for making calls no one saw. I was so embarrassed it became impossible for me to feel any sympathy for her, even when I'd see the looks other people in the stands shot her way. They didn't understand she was short-circuiting before their eyes. Although I did, I still didn't recognize that woman. She was a stranger to me.

I didn't want to talk about it. I didn't want to believe it. My greatest release was sports. Our junior high went up to ninth grade and when that year started for me George Corner was named the football coach. I was too small to play, not yet five feet tall or weighing even a hundred pounds. But I needed an activity, anything to keep me occupied, and George let me be on the team. I played end on offense and just ran around on defense. I wasn't very effective, and the kids were so huge it felt like my bones were shattering during every pileup.

One afternoon following an outburst from my mom, George asked me to come to his office after school. I thought I was going to be reprimanded or cut. But he just sat me down and asked, "How're things at home?"

"Cool," I said.

Then he deftly changed the subject and started talking about football, our season, how he was pleased with how well I was playing. He could sense that I was feeling more at ease and asked me, "How's your mom?" At first, I didn't respond, and he didn't push. He just waited. After a few more moments of silence, he practically whispered, "You can tell me."

"She's not so great," I answered. Then he told me his mom had suffered from mental disorders his entire life, and that he knew what I was going through. "You need to know that you're okay," he said. "You're not sick."

Naturally I felt relieved. He understood what I was worried about and what I was afraid of. Unfortunately, he couldn't make my mom feel better, too. Later that year I came home from school and my mom wasn't there. My father was, which was odd since his shift didn't end until 4:30, usually an hour or so after school let out. He told me my mom was sick, sick enough that she had to be taken to a hospital. She was okay physically, he said, but not mentally. Then he drove me out to see her.

They put the sickest patients on the sixth floor of the psychiatric hospital, the top of the building, and that is where my mom started. I sat in the common area, waiting to walk down the hall to see her. My palms were pressed together, sandwiched between my knees, and I was rocking back and forth in my seat, as though I were praying. A woman came up to me while I waited. She had garish red hair and mascara and lipstick painted onto her face and smeared. She sat down right next to me and started petting me, telling me how beautiful I was. It scared me to death. I didn't go back to visit until my mom was stable enough to be on the first floor.

She was in the hospital for a month and received several

rounds of electroshock therapy. It didn't work. One afternoon, a few weeks after she was released, I was walking home from school and, as I neared the bend in the road that came just before my house, I heard screaming. As I rounded the turn I saw my mom, twisting, turning, and trying desperately to get out of a straitjacket as two men from the hospital took her away. This time they tried treating her with insulin shock. When that failed they just put her on drugs. And that was that. She was hooked: She just drank her beer, smoked her cigarettes, took her drugs, and was just out of it. My father was always afraid she would pass out with a cigarette in her mouth and burn the house down. He was also livid that her drugs weren't covered by his insurance and their costs were draining the meager savings and college funds we had. And she wasn't even responsive. She just looked at him, at all of us, with these real thin cigarettes hanging from her mouth. She was my mom and I didn't even know her.

By the time I entered Interboro High School in 1961, I was just a pimply kid whom no one paid attention to, and was happy about it. I was trying to be faceless and nameless. I went out for the track team and made it, but had been spoiled by the precision and intensity of Marty Stern's practice. Everything he did had a purpose, which was to make us better runners. Even when we were circling Witmer Field, we felt that we were moving forward, that there was a lesson behind what we were doing. Nothing was done arbitrarily to satisfy a coach's whim or make him feel powerful and in control. That wasn't the case in high school.

The first week we just ran around the track at a slow pace.

I expected to excel. This was my sport. I needed it to unwind, be myself, and become engaged. But after that first week I skipped a day of practice. I couldn't take having to run in circles. When I went back the next day the coach asked me where I was and I just told him the truth: I was bored, I wasn't learning anything, and I wasn't sure I wanted to hang around. As any coach would, he told me I had a bad attitude and made the decision for me. He kicked me off the team.

He may have been right about my attitude. I had so much going on at home that I didn't know how to deal with, and that I didn't *want* to deal with. Sometimes, after school, I'd walk home across the football field, headed toward Glenolden Park. On a path between the football field and the baseball field was a small, eighteenth-century graveyard called Knowles Cemetery. The headstones were all tilted and the ground was uneven. A low-slung wall of smooth, round rocks surrounded the plots. I used to sit on the wall and think about how great it would be to get out of the project.

Then George Corner reentered my life. And saved it.

Between my junior and senior years at Interboro I grew three inches, going from five-three to five-six. And by then I weighed about 145 pounds. That same summer, George was named the new head coach of Interboro's football team. I hadn't played football since ninth grade—unless you count the games I imagined I played while cheering for the Eagles—but George invited me to come to a tryout camp in the Poconos. Actually, he didn't invite so much as expect me to be there. One day during the summer he saw me around town and said to me, "You're coming out for football this year, Vince." Before even thinking about it I answered, "You bet, coach."

It was a six-day camp, and those were the first six days I had ever been away from home without my parents. Every day seemed hotter than the day before. And every night was freezing. I showed up and saw all my classmates unrolling their sleeping bags on top of the mattresses in our cabins and realized I was in trouble. I didn't have a sleeping bag. So at night I put on all the sweats I brought with me and curled up in the fetal position to keep warm.

We woke up, ran a mile, ate breakfast, had a morning practice, had lunch, then a nap, then an afternoon practice, then dinner, then an evening practice, then spent an hour studying the playbook with the coaches. Not a minute was spared. It was physically brutal. All of our practices were on a pitched field, so half the time we were running uphill. Even after we were locked down in our cabin, George used to sneak around to make sure we weren't getting into trouble. One night he looked through the keyhole and saw us playing cards and gambling. The thing was, he never disciplined us. He figured as long as we weren't hurting ourselves there was no reason to punish us. But I never felt so free. I wanted to be a receiver and I figured this was my one chance to be Tommy McDonald. Every time I lined up in practice I said to myself, "I'm five-six, a hundred forty-five pounds, and I am Tommy McDonald, baby. Throw me the ball." I don't know where the confidence, in this setting, among guys who had played for two years already, came from. I had never had it before, had never done anything to build it up. But I was having so much fun. I just knew this was it.

George made Jim Haynie, a center the year before but a catcher on the baseball team, our new quarterback. In the Poconos, Haynie was just winging the ball, as if he were throwing it to second base. He and I just connected. I didn't know how to run a route; I just ran as hard, as fast, and as far as I could and Haynie would find me. I tried out for the team at the perfect time, playing for a new coach who believed in me and catching passes from a new quarterback who didn't have a favorite receiver yet. After the third day of camp George pulled me aside and said, "Holy cow, you can catch." He thought he was doing me a favor letting me try out, giving me an outlet to get away from my problems at home. But by the time we left the Poconos, George had redesigned his offense around me and Haynie.

We didn't have the biggest offensive line or the biggest defense. And all that anyone knew about our team was that George was a first-year coach, Haynie was a converted center, and the wide receiver was a pipsqueak. But we had an ultra-modern passing game, the slot offense, that had yet to be unveiled. Our first game was against Nether Providence, a school from an upscale town called Wallingford. The kids there grew up in huge homes built in the middle of dense forests. They never saw their neighbors, let alone heard them snore. They had a quarterback named Fred Ryder who would go on to the Naval Academy, and they should have had us beat before the game even started.

It was a beautiful, hot Saturday afternoon. The Interboro football stadium was packed. We could hear the fans murmur all the way down in our locker room, which felt as small as a dungeon. Before the game George told us to stay focused and not get caught up in the crowd. He had a soft, mellow voice, and he was always calm and never cursed. He kept us motivated by being positive, telling us matter-of-factly what we were going to do—that we would execute and that we would win. It seemed as though it was done before it even happened.

Of course, as we left the locker room and walked down a long, narrow tunnel toward the field, I forgot everything he told us. My legs felt heavy and I was so nervous I didn't think I was going to make it through the game. At one point while still in that dark hallway I told myself I didn't even want to be on the team anymore, because I was so afraid I would screw up and become a school joke. Then, as soon as we hit the sunlight, my attitude changed. It was wild to hear the band playing and to see the crowd. We warmed up and all I could think was that I was starting for my high school football team. I went from wanting to crawl under the bleachers to wanting everyone to see me, to recognize that I wasn't too small, that I could make it.

Before that game, and every other game the rest of the season, Haynie and I got together at my house to throw some warm-up passes in my backyard. Good thing, too, because George had us throwing as soon as we got the ball. I had five receptions that game, including one diving reception early in the game. But only one mattered. In the second quarter, we were already winning, and I ran a post pattern. During our practices George had emphasized the importance of selling the play-action fake. And Haynie was great at it because he had such big hands. As I sprinted down the field Haynie faked a handoff to the running back and then palmed the ball behind his back. The entire defense thought the back had the ball and gang-tackled him. Then Haynie stepped up into the pocket and hit me perfectly in stride. Once I had the ball and some room to roam, I was gone. We won the game 13–6. All of a sudden I mattered at Interboro High.

The season was full of highlights. We came back from two touchdowns down to beat Media High School. Late in the year, against Chi-Chester, I was double-teamed the entire game. Going into the fourth quarter we were losing and Chi-Chester became overconfident and stopped double-covering me. Then I scored the game-winning touchdown. We would go undefeated that season and have one tie, against Lansdowne Alden, a game in which I was hit so hard I was carried off the field with a concussion.

In the last game of the season, during Thanksgiving weekend, I had two touchdowns against Ridley Park. That was always the biggest game of the year for us, when the alumni were home from college and came to the game. I was in such great spirits after that, I felt like I had exploded and the kid that I had been in tenth and eleventh grade no longer existed. Even though I didn't play my first two years at Interboro, I earned honorable mention All-Delaware County. I didn't think how clichéd it was that I became popular only because I was a football player. Why would I? I had a pretty girlfriend named Sue Pendergrast, we called her Soupy, and we hung out all the time. She played Puck in *A Midsummer Night's Dream* and was a cheerleader. We were this idyllic high school couple. Kids I didn't know said, "Hi" and "Nice game" to me in the hallways. I had an identity that wasn't about being the kid whose mom was crazy, I was part of the fabric of the Interboro High community. Haynie and I hung out every weekend, taking our girlfriends to the dances they always had after football games. I was feeling pretty full of myself, actually. I had even taken the college boards and figured out what I would do with my life: I wanted to be a coach and a teacher, like George Corner. I applied to West Chester State College and was accepted. I began thinking that maybe I could get out of the project after all.

I had stopped worrying about what was going on at home, even though my mom had been hospitalized again. My father actually came down during a game, at halftime, to let George Corner know in case I didn't play well. When she got home she was stoned on her sedatives. And my dad continued to show his peculiar brand of support. Every day after his shift at Westinghouse ended he'd stop by the Interboro football field, watch practice for twenty minutes, then head home. By the time I got there an hour or so later he was usually asleep in his chair. My dinner would be in the oven and I'd eat it alone at the kitchen table.

Mostly I tried to stay out of the house as much as possible. The day after our game against Ridley Park the cheerleaders, players, and recent alumni met at Glenolden Park for an annual touch football game. Really, it was just an excuse for the guys to grope as many girls as possible without getting slapped. But on one play I got stuck at the bottom of a pile, with everyone's weight coming down hard on my wrist. I screamed out in pain and as people untangled themselves from on top of my arm I began to feel an intense throbbing. My wrist was shattered.

I was taken to the hospital and one of my friends must have called home, because when I got there my dad was waiting. He didn't say anything to try to comfort me, but it felt good that he was there. I needed surgery on the wrist, and I remember him walking with me beside the gurney toward the operating room. I had been shot up with anesthetic and could feel myself fading in and out of consciousness. I couldn't figure out what was real and what I was imagining and I started talking as if no one were around. Then I started screaming, "I hate you, Dad, I hate you, Dad, I hate my father."

I didn't see him standing there. I couldn't see anyone. I didn't even know what I had said until after the surgery, when I was in recovery, and a nurse told me. But I couldn't bring it up to him. And my father never said anything to me.

I GREW TWO more inches that fall and played on the basketball team, even starting while my wrist was still healing. I felt cool, and acted like it. Too cool, actually. One night I came home from a game and my father got all over me, telling me I was acting too smooth, that I was too full of myself. He said he was embarrassed to watch such a prima donna and that no son of his should play like that. It seemed harsh, unusually so. I was mad, but I also knew he was right, and I started to hustle and scrap and dive for every play. It would take me years to figure out my father's theories about raising children, that he wasn't trying to put me down so much as teach me to appreciate the opportunities I had, the ones he never got.

George Corner, meanwhile, had been named the new track coach. As basketball ended, he asked me to rejoin the track team, just to get into shape for baseball. I asked him what events he thought I should be in and he told me "Sprints and hurdles."

"What about pole-vaulting?" I asked.

"I can't let you," George said. "I talked to your dad and he told me if you do track and field I can't let you pole-vault because you might get hurt."

I complained and protested. I was pole-vaulting over the crick and clotheslines when I was seven years old, I told him. But George wouldn't give in. My father had gotten to him (my dad must have remembered that I also broke my arm pole-vaulting the crick when I was seven).

But just before track season began in March, George went to a weeklong football-coaching clinic in Atlantic City. While he was gone my friend Marty Houston and I decided to spend one afternoon screwing around with the pole vault. We went into the gym the day they were having cheerleading tryouts, so we tried showing off at first by warming up on the flying rings. Then we went out to the track, we set the bar, and took turns running down the ramp, planting our poles and flying.

At first I put the bar at nine feet, and I cleared it. Then I put it at ten feet, and I cleared that. Then I tried eleven feet, and I cleared that, too. That was the school record. And the only person who knew I could match it was Marty Houston. When George came back from his conference I pulled him into the gym and said, "Coach, I got to tell you something."

When I told him I could pole-vault, he started rubbing his face, acting nervous and concerned. He said no way, he promised my father. But I had no intention of leaving the track that day as anything but a pole-vaulter. Before George walked in I had already set the bar at eleven feet so I could demonstrate if I had to. So I grabbed a pole, sprinted down the runway, and flew high over the bar, easily clearing it and unofficially breaking the school record. Again.

"Okay," George said. "You can pole-vault. But we're not telling your father."

Of course, we both knew my father would find out. He had yet to miss a game I had ever played in. Sometimes he was late, but he was always there. Saying nothing. Sure enough, in our first meet, against Media High School, I was standing at the end of the runway, pole in hand, getting ready to sprint toward the bar, when I saw my father walk through the gate at the track. He looked at me as I got ready to pole-vault. He was wearing his blue Westinghouse work clothes and he still had small smudges of grease on his face and he was shooting me the angriest, sternest, dirtiest look. Before he could paralyze me with fear, I started running. And then I set the school record. My father didn't seem to have a problem with my pole-vaulting after that.

Later that season, at the Sharon Hill Relays, it became too dark to finish. The pole vault was the last event, and if we won that, we would win the meet. George begged the meet director to keep going and when he said it was too dark, George convinced him to line up all the cars in the lot with their headlights on and facing the pole-vault runway. Bathed in the light of a dozen cars, I leaped higher than anybody, twelve feet, four and a half inches. Later that year at the district championships I split my lip on a falling bar, went to the hospital for stitches, came back, pole-vaulted again, and finished first.

I won the county, suburban, and district pole-vaulting championships and came in fifth in the state. I never considered this as a way for me to go to college, but George did. He took me to visit Villanova, then LaSalle, then Temple. And they all dismissed me without even a glance, saying, "No thanks, we already got our guys." At least at Temple the coach, Jack St. Clair, was gracious. He said he'd love to have me, wished he'd known about me earlier, but he already had his guy, too. Then at a post-season all-star meet, called the Meet of Champions because it matched the top five pole-vaulters from Catholic, public, and suburban leagues, I beat all of those "guys." And still no scholarship came my way. I didn't take it as a slight. I was a late bloomer in football and track. Coaches had never heard of me, and by the time I had proven I wasn't a fluke, they'd locked up the athletes they wanted.

On Father's Day in 1964 I entered one more post-season all-star meet, which was held at LaSalle. All the guys I'd beaten at the Meet of Champions were there. And so were the coaches from the local colleges. This time, I not only won, I pole-vaulted more than fourteen feet and was just eighteen inches off the world record. That day I got offers from Villanova, Temple, and LaSalle. I told them no thanks, they should be happy with their guys. Instead I accepted a scholarship from St. Joseph's, the only school that hadn't turned me down, mainly because the coaches had never seen me. I was going to college on a track scholarship. I was an athlete.

After the meet, my father was actually happy. I got a hug. I think I saw a tear in his eye. He told me he was proud of me. He didn't say he loved me, but he did say he was proud.

FOUR

STARTED AT St. Joe's in the fall of 1964, but while I may have been moving on to college, it felt like I was taking a step backward. My scholarship covered tuition and books, but not room and board, which meant I had to live at home, not on campus. No one at school knew who I was, which put a pin in my ego after a senior year of high school that made me feel like the biggest little man on campus. And in those days freshmen weren't allowed to compete at the varsity level, which made it difficult to connect with my new teammates. St. Joe's was an all-boys school with a jacket-and-tie dress code, and I was coming from a co-ed school where most kids couldn't afford a jacket and tie. I felt like a sophomore in high school all over again, and I just wanted to survive the transition.

My ninety-minute commute to school began with a mile walk to the train in Upper Darby—which was west of

Philly—and then a transfer to a bus. Soon after school started I saw that friends from my neighborhood were occasionally making the same trek, and we started going to school together. It was comforting for all of us, since we felt so disconnected from the students on campus. We didn't go to St. Joseph's parties or bars, we mostly hung out together in Glenolden. It was like we were still in high school, only classes were harder.

I had always done the bare minimum required to get Bs while at Interboro. But when I got to college no one stayed on me to do even that. Instead of disciplining myself, I thought it was cool to have so much freedom and I rarely studied. Part of the problem was how much I hated my classes. Any hopes I had of being a teacher were quickly dashed. My coaches told me that my major would be Business and Marketing. The subject wasn't up for debate. Although they could have told me to major in religious studies, I wasn't paying any attention. Most of the time I was cutting classes to play basketball on the playgrounds in Glenolden or at the Interboro gym, waiting for the year to end so I could compete. I never considered I'd nearly flunk out.

That summer I needed a job for a new wardrobe and a new car. I couldn't keep commuting on the bus and train and go to practice, and I couldn't wear the same jacket and tie every day. My friends and I picked up the graveyard shift at National Rolling Mills, a ceiling-tile factory in Paoli, which was about twenty miles from Glenolden. From 12 A.M. to 8 A.M. we'd do quality control or pack the bars the ceiling tiles fit into. It was the eeriest feeling taking lunch at 3:30 in the morning, sitting in that picnic area underneath the lights. After work we'd find a bar, drink some beers, go home and crash for a few hours, get up early in the afternoon, have a few more beers, and go to work. But one hot morning after my shift ended, my mom started knocking on my door before I could fall asleep. I was surprised, because my mom had almost completely stopped interacting with us. She kept her cigarette in her mouth, her beer in her hand, and talked real slow, never losing the cig from between her lips. We could barely understand her. But when she opened the envelope, she looked as though she had had her fifteenth nervous breakdown. And I realized I had given it to her. She told me I had been sent a letter from St. Joe's that said I had failed out of school. My mom looked confused, like she didn't know what the letter meant and couldn't grasp the concept. Then, for just a flash, she was lucid and she promised me she wouldn't tell my father if I fixed it.

I called my coach, Louis NiCastro. I had liked him from the start, and not just because he gave me a scholarship when no one else would. He wasn't a screamer, just a paternal presence for everyone on the team. He called the athletic director, Jack Ramsey, who was also the basketball coach. (Jack would coach the Portland Trailblazers to the 1977 NBA title.) They both knew my situation at home was difficult because of my mom. And they arranged for me to get a second chance. That summer I took Accounting, Western Civilization, and Statistics, and

I passed. My dad wondered why I was taking so many classes during the summer. When I said I was trying to get ahead so I wouldn't be overwhelmed during track season, he just nodded his head as if he understood.

Our relationship had changed since high school. Maybe it's because he thought I was finally doing okay and that I hadn't wasted any of my gifts or opportunities. I had used sports to get ahead. For all either of us knew it could have been because of his criticism and my working hard to please him. Or maybe whatever I achieved was in spite of him. It might not have mattered to him. The end justified the means.

Or maybe he was no longer on my case because he was more exhausted than ever. He had scraped together some money to buy part of a Sunoco gas station with his youngest brother, Michael, and spent every night after his shift at Westinghouse working on cars there. At the end of the summer, he surprised me with a 1956 powder-blue Plymouth, which was loaded with the best parts he could afford from the local junkyard.

Which is why, for the first time, I felt bad when I lied to him about flunking out.

IN JANUARY 1965 President Lyndon Johnson was told by his advisers that the United States had reached a fork in the road regarding military involvement in Vietnam: The country either had to pull out what little personnel it had or completely commit. By that May, the first American combat-ready troops would arrive in the country. Two months later President Johnson would go on TV and say he was increasing the number to 125,000 troops and increasing the number of civilians drafted each month to 35,000. By August, opposition to the war was becoming so commonplace that Johnson signed a law criminalizing draft-card burning, making it punishable with a five-year prison sentence. Nobody really seemed to worry about it.

But I wasn't thinking about war or opposition to the war or burning a draft card. That summer I had started dating Janet Fitzgibbon, a girl who had been a couple of years behind me at Interboro. That winter I finally got to start competing in the indoor track season as a pole-vaulter and, occasionally, in some other events as well. Finally, I felt like a part of the St. Joe's community. We were a good, if not great, team. But we had great chemistry. The rivalries against the teams we competed against within the city were especially personal for me because of how I'd been spurned by those coaches in high school. One of our first dual meets that winter was against Temple, and Lou had me in the pole vault, long jump, triple jump, high hurdles, and leading off the 440 relay. I won the pole vault, long jump, triple jump, high hurdles, and my team won the 440 relay. Afterward I looked for Temple's coach, Jack St. Clair, and I said, "Coach, yo coach, remember me? I'm Vince Papale, the kid from Interboro."

"Boy do I," St. Clair said, laughing. "I have a feeling I will remember you every meet for the next three years."

Lou wasn't the kind of coach who got on his athletes to train harder. This wasn't high school, he reasoned, we were all adults and should know right from wrong and what needed to be done (something I didn't learn while failing out my freshman year). My sophomore year I figured out how to be self-motivated and take responsibility and I pushed my body to its limit. And then it broke.

For a long time the pole-vault pits were filled with sawdust, which didn't feel all that great when you landed on it back-first. But when I got to St. Joe's they started filling the pits with nets full of foam rubber. During one meet late in the indoor season, as I came down into the pit, my knee got caught on one of the nets. It was wrenched at an awkward angle and I could feel something tear. It wasn't a ligament—which could have sidelined me for good—but cartilage. And it required surgery. When I found out Jim Nixon, the Eagles' team doctor, was going to perform the surgery, I almost didn't mind going under the knife. That's how crazy I still was about the Eagles. I had just bought season tickets. I was actually proud that the team doctor was going to operate on me.

The rehab Dr. Nixon prescribed for my knee was largely weightlifting. I was still living at home, and it was hard for me to be on campus any longer than I had to while I was hobbling around. So, for one of the first times in my life, my dad showed me support and empathy. Using excess sheet metal that he picked up at Westinghouse, he created five-pound plates with holes in the middle. He brought several of them home and made a strap that I could fasten through the weights and around my ankle. I would sit on the edge of the kitchen table, with my legs dangling, and buckle the strap and weights to my ankle. Then I would lift, adding five pounds of weight for every set. At first the pain was excruciating and my knee felt weaker than a five-year-old's. But gradually, I became more comfortable and the pain subsided. Thanks to my dad, and a summer spent landscaping with my uncle Dom, I not only recovered, but I felt stronger when the next season rolled around.

That summer I also got to see my father in an entirely different way. My uncle Mike used a connection to get me a job delivering Pepsi products. Every morning I was up at 6 A.M., chugging this new soda Pepsi just put out called Mountain Dew. My father and Uncle Mike had bought the Sunoco together and whenever I was done driving the truck I'd go to the station and help them by pumping gas. I had never worked with my father and I saw how he laughed, how the people who brought their cars in to be fixed respected him. He was funny and carefree with his friends, in a way he never had been at home. I started to like him as a man.

By the next fall I felt like I belonged at St. Joe's. I drove a yellow Ford Fairlane station wagon with a V8 that sounded like a helicopter taking off. If the color didn't announce my presence, the pole-vault poles hanging through the window off the side of the car did. Vietnam was starting to become a little more real to us in 1966. Protests in a city filled with colleges were more frequent and with the draft in full swing, it felt closer to home. A lot of my friends on campus decided to join the Air Force ROTC. We romanticized the idea of flying one weekend a month, getting paid cash, and wearing sharp-looking uniforms while walking around campus. No one thought, I'm going to war if I take this step. I applied and, after passing the navigation exam, had an interview with a man named Captain Boyle. He stood real close to my face and stared hard, as though he were looking right through me. He asked me why I came to St. Joe's. I said because of a track scholarship. Suddenly he just exploded, as if I had told him the United States didn't belong in Southeast Asia. "You didn't think about the social life? You didn't think about academics?" I stammered out a "No sir" and he explained as loudly as possible that I wasn't fit for the Air Force if I couldn't come up with more thoughtful answers than that.

That wasn't my only confrontation with authority that fall. Coach NiCastro retired in the summer of 1966. His replacement was Kevin Quinn, a former track star at St. Joe's. The way Quinn approached managing the team made us feel as though we were nothing but a club team before his arrival. While we all loved Lou NiCastro, we didn't learn anything from him. He was a father figure, but when he was coach we didn't feel compelled to win. Quinn was the antithesis of NiCastro. He came in and told me I was done being just a pole-vaulter. He said I was gong to be a hurdler and sprinter and learn how to long jump on a regular basis, not just as a fill in. He sat us down and made it clear that he expected nothing less than a Middle Atlantic Conference Championship from his team. He was a disciplinarian who refused to let us finish a day unless he thought we were reaching our full potential. He modernized the St. Joe's track team, bringing in a weight trainer and coaches who focused on specific events. Suddenly, the intensity level of the program had been raised. It made it feel like it was more than just a hobby.

Quinn's first rule was that no one would be allowed to play basketball or football—which a lot of us did—because of the risk of injury. But pickup basketball and football games had helped me stay sane my freshman year—even if they did keep me from studying—and kept me in shape my sophomore year once I was through rehabbing my knee. I wasn't about to give them up.

One evening I went to the St. Joe's field to play in a pickup football game against guys from LaSalle. These games were usually covered by the local papers, with each one getting a small write-up. There was a writer there named Herm Rogul who became a Philly sportswriting legend. I knew him from my days at Interboro and from when he covered St. Joe's track meets. I saw Herm and told him, "You never saw me here tonight. If Quinn reads that I was playing he'll kick me off the team."

Naturally, the headline the next day read, "St. Joe's Track Star Papale Leads IM Team to Win." That day, Quinn suspended me for a week, during which time he beat me into the ground by making me run sprints and long distances but not letting me compete.

Our team was special that year, bonding on and off the

track. One of the seniors, a 440-relay runner and captain named Dave Van Dusen, was our social coordinator. Duse grew up in Lower Merion, on the Main Line, and it was a world I had never seen before. Every house seemed bigger than the next, with perfectly manicured lawns, two-car garages, and trees in the front yard that hid the mansions from the street. Duse became my confidante, taking me to parties with his friends, helping me fit in with people I thought I had no business talking to. As confident as I was as an athlete, I still felt inferior because I was so poor. But Duse just accepted me. When he got an apartment with some other seniors, he let me crash there every weekend, acting as if it were my own place. I was twenty-one years old, listening to the Doors, staying away from home, two-fisting pony bottles of Rolling Rock, and loving life.

It didn't hurt that I was doing so well athletically. I was winning dual meets against some of the top teams in the city and the conference in events I had never competed in before. In May 1967, we were expected to contend for the title at the Middle Atlantic Conference Championships, which we had never won before. Coach Quinn expected me to lead the way. I was the team's top triple jumper, pole-vaulter, long jumper; the second-best high hurdler; and led off the 440 relay. The week before the MAC Championships, at the Quantico Relays, Coach Quinn told me to just concentrate on pole-vaulting; he wanted me fresh for the next weekend. On my first warm-up vault, as I landed, my ankle rolled over. I felt it pop out of place and I fell to the ground as though I'd been shot, grabbing my ankle and screaming out in agony.

Back in Philly, I met with Jim Nixon, the Eagles' team doctor who had repaired my knee. He was a really calm, straightforward man with a ring of gray hair surrounding his balding head.

"Your ankle is shot," he told me. "What do you have coming up?"

"I have the MAC Championships," I said.

"Impossible," he responded. "If you compete, don't even bother coming back to me. I don't want to see you."

But I couldn't accept that as an answer. On the morning of the meet, our trainer taped up my right ankle so tight I thought I'd lose whatever feeling I had left. But again, as I tried a practice vault, my ankle gave out at the end of the runway. I was crushed. It was my time to shine, I thought, and I blew it. As I sat crying on a bench next to the runway, Teddy Quedenfeld, the Temple trainer, tried consoling me. He took me back to the trainers' room, gave me a towel to wipe my face, and asked me what one event I thought my ankle could handle. I told him the long jump, which was the shortest run and put the least amount of impact on the joint. St. Joe's didn't have the budget for a full-time trainer. The best we could do was a student, who was good for ice packs and pain medicine and taping, but nothing more serious than that. But Teddy was a pro who saw how upset I was and, in the spirit of sportsmanship, tried helping me. He pulled out a splint, no more sophisticated than a couple of Popsicle sticks, and taped it tight to both sides of my ankle. I jogged around for a minute, but was wary of trying too much. It was either going to work or not, but I didn't want to find out while I was warming up in the trainers' room.

As I neared the point where I'd have to make my jump I stutter-stepped, so I could leap off my opposite foot. Imagine being a right-handed pitcher who's asked to make the game-winning pitch with your left hand. That's how awkward it felt as I took off. More than twenty-two feet later I came down to earth. My dad had been standing at the end of the runway and he couldn't stop hugging me, telling me how proud he was of me. The guys were mobbing me. My jump was the last one of the day, and it had clinched the MAC title.

That night, I took Duse and all the guys to the project to celebrate. It was the first time I had invited someone over since my mom's visit to the state hospital. But I didn't think I had anything to be ashamed of anymore.

MY SENIOR YEAR, we won the MAC title again, and I set a conference record for the most points in the conference championship meet by winning the long jump, triple jump, and 440 relay, and by placing third in the hurdles and second in the pole vault. The performance helped me earn a share of St. Joe's senior athlete of the year award with basketball star Billy D'Angelis. And my point total in the conference championship meet set a record that will never be broken, because the Middle Atlantic Conference disbanded in 1974.

Although my senior year was going so well athletically, after Duse left following my junior year, it felt like I had left my social life in Neverland. I didn't have a Philly pad to crash at. I didn't know anyone having parties on the Main Line. Instead, my senior year I spent weekends back in Glenolden, going out with Janet, believing that, someday soon, the military was going to want me.

N 1968, if you were twenty-two years old and in great physical condition, you were going to Vietnam. It was silly to even consider grad school or careers or what we wanted out of life after college. We assumed we'd get eaten up by the Army for two years, fall off the map into some place in Southeast Asia we couldn't pronounce, and then get on with the rest of our lives. We didn't think we were going to die, but our futures weren't our own.

While waiting for what I assumed was the inevitable, my sister, a teacher at Ridley High School, suggested I apply there, if for no other reason than teachers were getting draft deferments. But it made sense for me. I had always considered being a teacher. The most important influences in my life had been coaches and teachers and I wanted to have an impact like that. Besides, I didn't plan on using the business degree

St. Joe's forced on me. I applied to Interboro, too, thinking it was a long shot. But they did, in fact, have an opening. And wham, in September 1968, after a summer spent earning my teaching certificate at St. Joe's, I began teaching Accounting, Business Law, and Consumer Economics to juniors and seniors at Interboro High. (Guess that business degree helped after all.) I was also named the football coach for the junior high school's under-100-pound team. George Corner, still the high school coach, oversaw the high school and junior high football program, which meant I was working in his system. He mentored me on how to be a football coach. And I thought it was the greatest thing that had ever happened to me. I was working at the feet of the man I admired most, the man I loved like a father, sometimes more than my own father. I wanted to do this for the rest of my life.

The teaching was a lot harder than I expected. I was twenty-two, three months out of college and just four years out of high school. Half the kids I taught had brothers or sisters I was friends with growing up. They had a hard time seeing me as their teacher. And I had a harder time being one. I was too idealistic. I wanted to be their friend by treating the classroom like a democracy, and they ran all over me. I had no control. That first year of teaching I lost ten pounds because I was so nervous every day.

After a year in the high school, I switched to ninth graders at the junior high. From the beginning, I was a disciplinarian. I acted like that for one year in the classroom and never had any kids act out again.

As I became more comfortable with myself, the kids could see that I understood, or at least remembered, what it was like to be young and confused and hate your parents. In the late 1960s, that described nearly every teenager in the United States. I taught a typing class and tried to teach the kids to learn to type to the beat of Santana's "Black Magic Woman" and "In-A-Gadda-Da-Vida" by Iron Butterfly. I still don't know if any of them learned to type, but they can keep time to the beat. I let kids come into my classroom during lunch and play music and relax in ways they couldn't anywhere else. I drove a 1967 Mustang and as I approached school I would always rev my engine or grind my gears, so the kids sneaking cigarettes in the parking lot knew I was coming. I wasn't trying to be their best friend, but I was a confidante. They came to me for advice when they were in a jam, especially when it came to drugs. If they couldn't talk to their parents or needed help or thought they were going to lose it, they could give me a call at home. Because I was from the neighborhood, and still lived there, I felt a tremendous responsibility to these kids.

In the spring of 1969 George Corner retired as the track coach. And he asked me to replace him. This was near the end of my first year of teaching, and any discomfort I still felt in front of the classroom melted during practice. I never second-guessed myself and never worried about being friends with my athletes. Maybe I felt I knew I could teach them something; I was still better at most events than they were, so I never had to make them like me to earn their respect. Our first week of practice was during Easter break and three seniors decided to test me by not showing up for practice. I knew I had to suspend them, but I went to George for advice, and he agreed. Otherwise, he said, it would only get worse. They were my best athletes, but I dressed them down in front of the entire team and told them if they did it again they'd be kicked off the team. They practiced the rest of that week, but during our first meet of the year, against Ridley High, they kept score and raked the pits for their teammates. We lost the meet by two points. But I never had any more problems.

That would be the only meet we'd lose all year. We were an efficient, well-trained team. My assistant coaches, Tom Robinson, Bill Gross, and Jamie Nachman, and I tried to implement techniques and training methods that seemed untraditional at the time but were just starting to catch on in colleges. It was one of the benefits of coaching after being so recently removed from competing. We made all the shot-putters and javelin throwers do the running sprinters had to do, and all the sprint guys endured the high-intensity weight training the field guys did. It made everybody get in better shape, but it also fostered camaraderie among the athletes. No one got out of anything, everyone suffered the same. In the early 1970s, I'd incorporate downhill training into their regiment as well. I had read that the great Russian sprinter Valeri Borzov—who'd win the gold in the 100 meter and 200 meter at the 1972 Olympics—sprinted downhill during his workouts. Lucky for me, I had the steep hills of Glenolden Park in the school's backyard. First I would have my athletes stride slowly downhill so they could get comfortable and learn how to balance while letting gravity pull them down. Then I would have them sprint uphill to improve the strength in their quads and legs. Then they'd go back downhill at half speed, then again at three-quarter speed and again at full speed. Having to control themselves as they ran on a slope helped them naturally lengthen their strides. By the time they were on flat ground, they were getting an extra couple of feet with every step.

I also stole a little something from Marty Stern in the way we handled the baton. The old way had been to have the runner receiving the baton begin sprinting and pump with one arm while the other went stiff behind him, waiting for the transfer. But Marty taught us to keep both of our arms pumping. The man handing the baton off learned to time his release with when one of our arms made its backswing. When he was ready to transfer, he'd yell "Bucs," which was the name of our team.

We were all about intimidation and psyching out opponents before the meet started. Our warm-ups were black hooded sweatshirts with BUCS emblazoned across the front in gold. And we'd walk onto the track with the hoods over our heads and tightly tied. Then we'd do our pre-meet stretching in total silence, all in sync, changing from one stretch to another without so much as a whistle blown. The guys on our relay would run around the track in a single file of four, passing the baton back and forth between them, from front to back and back to front, without saying anything other than "Bucs" whenever the baton changed hands. They looked like perfectly trained soldiers.

We were so dominant we used to use some meets as training exercises. Sometimes we'd have our sprinters take turns shot-putting or our shot-putters run the 100-yard dash. By my second season coaching, the track team was undefeated and won the county championship. I was voted the youngest ever president of the Delaware County Track Coaches Association.

Shortly after George named me track coach Janet pushed me to train for the decathlon in the 1972 Olympics. We were married in February 1969, and she could tell early on in the track season that I missed the competition. I woke up early, trained, came home to work on my lesson plans, went to school still in my sneakers, and then worked out some more with my kids during practice. I even turned the extra bedroom in our apartment into a gym so the kids had a place to exercise when the school was closed.

I was always pushing them to beat the records I had set when I was at Interboro. And I tried to keep practices interesting. Some days we'd skip running at the school or in Glenolden Park and go into the gym to blast an album by the Doors or Queen's "We are the Champions" and play bombardment. We had one group of kids, distance runners, that were so much smarter than me I couldn't communicate with them. They knew it and they teased me constantly. I just called them the motherfuckers, or muffs for short, and had T-shirts made that read MUFFS across the front.

Life seemed pretty good from the outside. I was a football and track coach and lived in a two-bedroom apartment near a park that had a gazebo in it. My friends Chuck Gardner and

Billy Thomas and I bought season tickets to the Eagles games at Franklin Field in the fall of 1969. Chuck had been my best friend since junior high. He was the only guy I had no problem bringing over to see my mom after she got really bad. He'd come in, call her Al, give her a big hug, and act as if nothing was odd about her behavior. Most people back then just didn't know how to act around someone who was mentally ill. One summer we took Chuck to the shore with us for a vacation. We'd play football on the beach and for this, Chuck was the perfect partner. He liked to stand in one place, stay clean, and just throw the football as far as he could. I wanted to dive, get sandy, and run until I passed out. One afternoon Chuck unloaded a beautiful, tight spiral. I was sprinting and kicking up sand, keeping my eye on the ball as it arced through the sky. I was oblivious to everything around me. As the ball reached my fingertips I didn't hear Chuck screaming, "Look out, look out!" An older lady had stood up in my path just as I was about to catch the ball. And I flattened her. As soon as we saw she was alive, we ran from that beach as if the tide were about to swallow us up. It's one of the few times I saw Chuck move that fast.

I was always the jock and Chuck was always the worker. As a kid, he got up early every morning for a paper route. While most of our friends were at practice after school, Chuck tried to find ways to earn money. His dad was a shift worker, too, only he worked overnight and Chuck never saw him. He was one of the few friends I had who was envious of the relationship I had with my father. Chuck just thought it was nice he was around. When we graduated from high school he worked for the railroad for five years. Then, the year we bought Eagles tickets, he got a job selling women's shoes at Baker's Shoe Store in Delaware County.

Billy Thomas worked in the post office, and he was the only guy I knew who got as happy as I did when fall came around every year. When we were in high school, he grew up across the street from Interboro and as school started and the season drew near, we'd walk to his house and sit on his lawn talking about how happy the Eagles made us. And this was a couple years after the championship in 1960, when they were never winning more then three or four games in a season.

For about $100 apiece, the three of us bought nosebleeds in Franklin Field's upper deck. We'd take the train from Secane, Delaware County, right to Franklin Field and when we got off, there was always a crush of people bottlenecked at the stadium entrance. Franklin Field was originally built in 1895, reconstructed in the mid-1920s, and held more than fifty thousand people. It was built straight up, so even from the highest level it felt and looked as if you were right on top of the field. There was one problem: All the bathrooms were on the lower level of the stadium.

Chuck was five-eleven and a stringbean of a guy, and he had incredible balance. He joked that he got it from having to put together the storefronts at Baker's and maneuver through all the displays showing off pumps and Mary Janes. One bad move and they'd all come tumbling down. When we'd get near the stadium entrance Chuck would say, "Get on my hip."

He'd weave his way through the crowd better than any of the Eagles ever did.

The Eagles of the 1960s were a sorry bunch. After that championship season Van Brocklin and the coach, Buck Shaw, retired. Bednarik only played two more seasons. In 1964 the Eagles traded Tommy McDonald to the Cowboys for three players, including a kicker. They'd win just three games in 1962, just two in 1963, and finish out the decade with one winning season, in 1966. When we bought our tickets three years later we were partially doing it so we could yell at the players in person instead of wasting our breath doing it at the television.

That same fall I was invited by Bill Gross to play in a rough touch football league that played on Sunday mornings. Everyone out there had played high school football and was using the league as an excuse to relive their glory days. And I was no exception. After the games, still sweating and in my rough touch team T-shirt, I'd grab a pint of blackberry brandy, meet Bill and Chuck on the train, ride his hip to our seats, and scream until I was hoarse. Chuck used to joke with me that he thought I could do better than the guys on the field. Inside, I thought he was right. I wanted the team to do something—anything— that would make me want to come back again. Of course they never did. And I came back anyway.

I WAS HAVING so much fun coaching, teaching, playing rough touch, and going to Eagles games I had almost completely forgotten about the Army and Vietnam. But they hadn't forgotten about me. I received a draft notice shortly after school began. It seemed Interboro had neglected to send in the paperwork required for me to get a deferment as a teacher.

By 1969 Vietnam was a full-fledged war, both in Southeast Asia and at home. While it had seemed like something inevitable—but doable—when I was in college, it seemed frightening now. So much had changed for me in the year since I stopped being a college student. Janet and I got married, for one. And I was no longer adrift, wondering what I would do until the Army had its way with me. I had found a career that I loved, that I didn't want to give up. I had a future. I wasn't against the war—I never protested—but I wasn't for it either. I wasn't very political. I just wanted to be happy and successful and had a job that made me feel that way. I didn't want that taken away from me.

A week before my draft physical I was playing a pickup game of basketball with a bunch of teachers at the Interboro gym. We had a weekly game, every Thursday, and afterward we would go to Benny's Bar for a few drinks, which usually meant closing the place down. On Friday those teachers who had gone out the night before usually gave their kids a study hall or quiz, and all the kids could see in our eyes why. In that game before my physical I went up for a rebound and landed awkwardly on the same ankle I had dislocated in college. I had to be helped off the floor.

A week later, I showed up at my draft physical on crutches with a dislocated ankle. The physician gave me a six-month deferment. Then he saw my wedding band and asked me how long I had been married. When I told him I was a newlywed he gave me another six-month deferment. He promised I'd be reclassified and have to come back when my number was called again. But no one ever called me. By accident and luck, I had escaped the Vietnam War.

THE IRONY WAS that, though I was a newlywed, the Army doc wasn't doing Janet and me any favors by giving us six more months to spend together. We threw parties at our place, where she drank whiskey sours and I drank beer, and we appeared to be a happy couple. But almost as soon as we got married, I thought I had made a mistake. We didn't love each other, not the way people getting married should. Our relationship was platonic. But our friends were getting married and I thought I was going to Vietnam and being with her was comforting. For all the wrong reasons, we stayed together when we should have broken up.

We were married in February 1969 at a church in Springfield and then had the reception on a Saturday afternoon in Chester. Chuck was my best man. It was just my high school buddies, her friends, and our parents. Her dad was a bartender who found some ways to make money on the side. They lived in a nice house on a cul-de-sac and paid for the wedding. My parents, meanwhile, got us the best gift they could afford: a linoleum-topped kitchen set. Janet and her parents hated it because it looked so cheap.

As soon as we got married, everything I did seemed to annoy her. I was no longer a track star whose name was in the newspapers, I was just a schoolteacher making less money than she was as an executive secretary. I liked to play rough touch football on the weekends and she'd say, "Come on, Vince, when are you going to grow up and stop playing this game?" She'd get irritated that I was gone all Sunday afternoon with Chuck and Billy at Eagles games instead of being at home working on making the apartment look nice. And she hated my relationship with the kids on the team and at school. Part of it was her being jealous, part of it was the fact that they came over a lot to work out, which I guess would annoy anyone. But I was committed to teaching. She just saw me as a guy with Peter Pan syndrome who was wasting his time at a dead-end job.

By our second year of marriage we were really drifting apart. She was not a sports fan and rarely came to our track meets, and even when she did come she seemed preoccupied afterward, as though she couldn't wait to get as far away from the track as possible. After that 1970 season I decided to get my master's in counseling from West Chester State. If I was going to be giving these students advice I didn't want to be making mistakes. And I continued to train every day for the decathlon. Janet meanwhile got a job working for the Philadelphia director of the United Way. Between the two of us—with me training for the decathlon, coaching track, teaching classes, and taking classes and her working hard at her new job—we never saw each other.

In the fall of 1971 I had moved up from coaching the junior high football team to being an assistant to George with the high school team. Working side by side with George, seeing him as a teacher dealing with kids and not as the kid looking for his guidance I had once been, only convinced me more of his humanity and kindness. Football is a sport where coaches rely on belittling their team players, no matter what level, to make them stronger. But George never did that. He never had to. His guys didn't want to let him down, and more than that, they feared how they'd feel if they did.

After one game early during the 1971 season I came home, opened the door, and yelled, "Hey honey, we beat Chester." But there was no answer. I looked around and the place was empty, completely cleaned out of all but necessities and a note taped to one of the walls. It read: "You'll never go anywhere, never make a name for yourself, and never make any money." That was it. She had nothing else to say to me.

I just cried. I sat in the apartment and cried for days. I had no furniture, no savings to buy furniture, and couldn't afford the rent on just my salary. I had known the marriage was over almost from the day it started, but my parents had been miserable for years and never divorced. I just never saw splitting up as an option; somehow I thought we were going to work it out. And I never considered what it would actually be like if my marriage ended.

After those first forty-eight hours I got myself together and went home to my parents. I had nowhere else to go. I dreaded seeing my father. While we'd become closer, I still craved his ever-elusive approval. I told him that Janet had left me, that I was broke, and that I needed money, which I knew he couldn't spare. I expected criticism and a lecture on what I had done wrong. Instead he gave me as much as he could and simply said, "I never liked her much anyway."

SIX

ANET'S LEAVING me was bad. And things would get even worse. I had been training at Widener College to try out for the decathlon in the 1972 Olympics for almost two years. I was up early in the mornings taking long jogs, working the machines in our apartment, and then competing hard with my kids after school. I had exhausted my eligibility at St. Joe's, so to keep in competition shape I entered all-comers meets all over the city. Anyone could compete in these meets, high school, college, Amateur Athletic Union (AAU), or independents like me.

I had been aiming to compete in the Drake Relays, in the spring of 1972, and the Penn Relays a couple of weeks later. Placing well in those would make me eligible to compete in the Olympic Trials in the summer, just before the games. But my request to participate in the Drake Relays was denied in one of the most condescending letters I'd ever received. They didn't just deny me the chance to compete. The organizers made fun of my experience and wondered why they would let a nobody who was four years out of college and had never participated in any serious decathlon competition join in what they considered their prestigious meet. I felt worthless and low and as though I had wasted nearly three years of my life training for nothing. A couple of weeks later I received news about the Penn Relays. The organizer of the relays was Jim Tuppeny, the former Villanova coach who couldn't be bothered with me when I was in high school. Through a friend of Tuppeny's I was told that amateurs who had exhausted their college eligibility and were petitioning to compete as independents wouldn't be invited to the Penn Relays. Tuppeny's friend told me that the NCAA was giving the Penn Relays a hard time about members of the AAU and the NCAA lining up against one another.

I believed what I was told and never bothered to investigate if it was true on my own. I accepted my fate—it wasn't meant to be. But the day after the Penn Relays I read about AAU athletes who had competed and realized I had been blackballed from the meet. I blamed myself more than anyone else. I should have spoken up or looked into the alleged new policy. Instead I accepted what I was told and gave up on my dream. I vowed I would never do that again.

Without competing in at least one of those two relays my chances at being invited to the Olympic tryouts, however small they were, disappeared. Within seven months my wife left me and it seemed my athletic career was over. I took the letter from Janet and the letter from Drake and put them on the wall. I called it my "I'll show you" wall. But it would take a while before I felt strong enough to prove anything to anyone. I was shattered.

FOR THE FIRST time since my senior year in high school, I had no reason to train. My only outlet for competition now was the rough touch football league. This wasn't your typical, Sunday-in-the-park-with-your-buddies kind of league. Forget the images of the Kennedys tossing the ball on the beach and playing family games in Hyannis Port after lunch. The emphasis was on *rough,* not *touch,* and it was a game that was unique to Philly and Delaware County. Rough touch football was as much a part of our area as cheesesteaks. So much so that Philly native Bill Cosby made it a part of his routine. He explained that the usual play call in a North Philly huddle went something like this, "Take seven steps, cut behind the blue Buick, run into my grandmother's house, go out the back door, take the 23 trolley, get off at Eighteenth Street, and I'll fake it to you." The *Philadelphia Inquirer* described rough touch players as "guys who go to Pat's Steaks and scream in frustration at the Eagles on Sunday afternoon."

All the teams were sponsored by local taprooms, and the games became big draws for the bars. There'd be fans lined up on the sides of these high school fields drinking from cases of beer one of the bars brought along, and then afterward we'd go back to party at the bar until it was time to go to the Eagles game. Or sometimes we'd just stay there all day. The first year I played was in 1969, for Cannon's Café in Eddystone near Widener University, which was where the Eagles had training camp. Eddystone was a real lower-middle-class, blue-collar community on the Delaware River. We'd go out all night on Saturday and sometimes show up at the games hungover— or maybe still somewhat drunk. Then we'd beat the hell out of one another.

Rough touch is seven-on-seven, everyone is eligible. The center underhand-tosses the ball to the quarterback, two guys stay in to block, and two rushers come in full speed on every play. No one counts one-Mississippi, two-Mississippi. The rushers just go. The tags are a forearm to the face or an elbow to the side, or just full-on tackles. These were battles for pride. It may have been Cannon's Café vs. Benny's Bar, but it might as well have been Interboro vs. Ridley. Whatever rivalries we had in high school still existed, only they felt stronger. It felt like pure hatred. These games were how we took out our frustrations for the week. Sometimes it seemed we had more fights in the league than we had touchdowns. We used to joke that if you really wanted to train for DelCo rough touch football, go down to Acapulco and dive off the cliffs. No fair aiming for the water.

And we all took it seriously, no matter what state of inebriation many were in when we showed up to play. Teams recruited the best talent in their town. There was a group of officials who kept stats on the games. Roster changes were

regulated. There was even a waiver wire. Ambulances and police were always there.

I felt like a marked man when I played because I wasn't too
far removed from my days at St. Joe's. The *Delaware County
Daily Times* covered rough touch games and I got written up a
lot. Which cost me. That first year I was playing for Cannon's
Café and led the league in receiving and made the all-star
team. But I also broke my nose, my ribs, and had a few teeth
knocked loose. That was the cost of playing. I'd kick off and
then run down to make the touch. One time I didn't pick my
head up in time and, *pow,* Tony Daliessio and Jimmy Joyce si-
multaneously hit me so hard I landed flat on my back. But
I lived for those games, especially after my marriage ended.

In 1971, the fall that Janet left me, I started playing for
Max's, a taproom on Chester Pike in Prospect Park. Max's was a
smoky little hole with a shuffle bowl table and a pinball machine that all the girls liked to play when they wanted to get
our attention. Max was a gentle old Hungarian. But his daughter Maxine, well, you didn't want to mess with Maxine. We
played on a field behind a rock-and-roll joint called the T-bar.
The field was made of rocks, broken beer bottles, and small
patches of grass. Bill Gross—one of my assistant track coaches
and the guy who had introduced me to rough touch—was on
the team. Jimmy Scott was one of the other receivers, and he
ended up having a tryout with the Dallas Cowboys. Not all of
the rough touch guys were washed-out high school jocks or
thugs looking for a fight. Some of us could actually play. And
that just made things worse for us out on the field.

It didn't matter how many concussions I got or bones I broke, even in the rough touch league I had a rep as a track star turned football player. Which meant other players thought I was soft. Guys used to tell me they could tell I didn't like getting hit, that I didn't want to make a tackle. If I had made every tackle in a game I'd still hear that I would rather run around a guy than through him, which was the most mortal sin you could make in DelCo rough touch football.

After one game a bunch of us went back to Benny's Bar to have a few beers. This was in the fall of 1973. I was still working on my master's at West Chester and was dating a real foxy babe and lighting it up in rough touch, so I thought I was doing okay in life. I was getting my confidence back after a couple of years of being beaten down. While standing at the bar a tough thug from the project named Johnny Moran started giving me a hard time. We were about the same age, and Johnny also had been a good athlete while we were growing up, so we had always had a bit of a rivalry. While I was playing rough touch, he was playing semi-pro football for Tinicum AC, the same team my dad had played for. He was drunk, and I had had a few, and he started calling me a wimp and accused me of being a cocky hotshot athlete. He told me that if I were that tough and that good I would play semi-pro, not rough touch on Sunday mornings. We were in our mid-twenties, but not all that much had changed since we were seven years old and playing monkeyball in the project. It didn't matter what kind of jobs we had, if we had kids, good marriages, or if we were serving the community. All of our credibility, our reputations, still hinged on how tough we were and what kind of athletes we were. I was a teacher getting my master's in counseling, trying to convince my students to walk away from confrontations like these, that they didn't have to accept every challenge to their manhood that some jerk presented to them.

But I couldn't help but respond to Moran. I wasn't going to fight him. I just looked across the bar and said, "Screw you, Moran. I'm going to try out for a semi-pro team and I'll probably become one of the best receivers in the league." I guess decking him would have had more impact. But at least now I had a challenge to shoot for, because if I didn't make it in semi-pro ball, I'd never be able to show my face at Benny's again.

THE ASTON KNIGHTS were our local semi-pro team, located on the Delaware border about ten miles from where I lived. They played in the Seaboard League, which stretched from Hartford, Connecticut, to Portsmouth, Virginia, with teams in Hagerstown, Maryland; Hempstead, New York; and Chambersburg, Conshohocken, and Ridley Township, Pennsylvania. The Knights were known as a particularly tough team, loaded with ex-college players, including John Waller, the former Temple quarterback; Frank Ryan, a running back from Duke; Mike Kondrla, an ex–Notre Dame linebacker; and Jack Hess, an Interboro alum and former standout linebacker at Princeton. The year before I tried out everyone in the Seaboard League feared this one kid no one had ever seen before named Jimmy Jones. He was a defensive tackle listed as a grad of Poland University. The man had speed and strength and made everyone he played against look as though they were standing in stone. So few people knew who he was that a couple teams thought he was some high school player who had been kicked off or quit his team and changed his name so he could play. They were right. Jimmy Jones was Joe Klecko, a kid from Chester who would go on to star at Temple during the next four years, win two NCAA heavyweight boxing club titles, and become an All-Pro defensive lineman with the New York Jets.

The Knights had a tryout on a hot night in the middle of the summer at Sun Valley High School, where they played their home games, and which didn't look as nice as it sounded. It was never sunny, and there was no valley. But the Sun Oil Company refinery nearby had put up the money to build the field. It may have been one of the first naming rights deals in sports. I pulled into the parking lot in a 1967 Mustang convertible, four on the floor with dual shocks. It was Eagles green, of course. And the top was down. To everyone there I probably looked like some kind of lightweight looking to play with the big boys, and no doubt made myself a target once practice started. My potential teammates had no idea how scared I really was. Driving in I asked myself, Oh man, what am I doing here? Did I really just do this on a dare? Because some idiot in a bar challenged me to try out for a freaking semi-pro team? That's exactly what I was thinking.

The first guy I noticed was Phil Pompilli, the coach, who made Bill Parcells look like Twiggy. I was wearing raggedy shorts and the team-issued shoulder pads and helmet. As I looked around, I didn't think I looked to be in any worse or any better shape than the other fifty guys standing there. Pompilli lined us up as best he could and told us to run around the field to get warmed up. I'm thinking, You gotta be kidding me. My first chance to make an impression is going to be running around the field. That's perfect. As soon as he blew the whistle I started sprinting around the field. I'm sure the other guys hated me even more now, but I wasn't there to make friends. I needed to make the team. I was forty yards ahead of the pack when I finished circling the field, pulling up exactly where Pompilli was standing.

Then Pompilli broke us down position by position and I lined up with the other wide receivers for pass-catching drills. While standing there I saw that the quarterback was John Waller, who had gone to Ridley High School when I was at Interboro. Delaware County was pretty provincial, and the feelings we had for high school rivals didn't fade easily. We had all been in school in the late 1950s and early 1960s, when school pride meant everything. So, naturally, John Waller and I hated each other, even though we'd never said more than a handful of words to each other before that day.

Then he threw me that first ball. It was perfect, as if someone had tied a string from his hand to mine and ran the ball along the length of it. Every pass for the rest of that tryout looked and felt the same. We were in perfect rhythm. When

I made the team Pompilli told me I'd get paid a pair of Riddell cleats to start the season, $50, and a six-pack of beer after every game.

I relished being on this semi-pro team because I was a football player. That was the greatest thing in the world to me. I was so proud of that. I loved having black and blue marks and having my elbows all skinned up. To be honest, I did worry about the contact before I started playing. Then it became an instinctive response: You see a guy with the ball and you want to hit him. I loved playing under lights at Sun Valley on Saturday nights, which was the first time I had ever competed at night, not counting the time George Corner made everyone turn their car lights onto the track at the Sharon Hill Relays.

Mostly, I loved running post and fly patterns with pads on. It felt different from the rough touch leagues—and not just because the talent was better and I wasn't unprotected while people tried to maim me. It felt legitimate, with schemes and coaches and guys who played because they wanted to compete and win, not because they were pissed and looking to take out a week's worth of frustration. We played well that year, advancing to the title game. But it was the game against Hagerstown that would spin my life in a different direction. Hugh Wyatt, a Yale grad who had quit the corporate rat race to become a football coach, coached Hagerstown. They were one of the Seaboard League's perennial powers, but that day Waller and I were unstoppable. He hit me ten times, including three touchdowns. All three were deep passes—two posts and a fly—where I just ran by the defensive backs as though they were stuck in cement.

A few months after that game, with the season over, I got a call from Phil Pompilli. It was May 1974 and I was still teaching and coaching at Interboro, taking classes toward my master's, bartending on weekends to make extra cash, and dating a former Miss Delaware. At this point in my life I felt like I was on a pretty straight path: I'd finish my graduate degree, teach junior high school, play semi-pro football, go to Eagles games, and maybe someday get married again. I didn't have any aspirations that were greater than that. Other than playing for the Eagles, which was a pipe dream I didn't really take too seriously. I had sent them a letter after that first semi-pro season, but I never heard anything from them. And, in reality, I didn't need anything more than what I had. This was the life for me. I was having fun and just very comfortable with it all.

I assumed Phil was calling to talk about next season. Instead, he was calling with an invitation. A new professional football league was being formed and would begin play that July, in just twelve weeks. Philadelphia had been awarded a franchise. It was called the World Football League (WFL), the team was the Bell, and Philly's director of player personnel was Hugh Wyatt, whose Hagerstown Bears I had made to look like statues. He asked Phil to find me and make sure I attended the tryout that weekend in Cherry Hill, New Jersey, a posh suburb outside Philly that I had never heard of.

When I arrived at the high school football stadium I

thought it was going to be an intimate workout. Instead, I saw six hundred other guys, preening during the warm-ups, trying to impress coaches and scare off the competition. A lot of them were wearing football pants and football jerseys. But all I had was a pair of Interboro sweats and the Riddells I'd been given while playing for Aston. I saw the quarterback King Corcoran, a local semi-pro star who played for the Pottstown Firebirds. His claim to fame was completing three passes for the AFL's Boston Patriots in 1968. King was talking to the coach, Ron Waller (no relation to John), a Delaware legend.

Waller was not unlike me when he first started playing football: A kid who was deemed too small, but by dint of luck and a growth spurt, he was given an opportunity. Growing up he was an overweight kid who loved sports. His friends used to tease him that the only way he'd ever get to second base was by hitting a home run. But just before high school he grew from five-five to five-ten and became a lean 170 pounds. As a freshman he was the backup quarterback, and he earned the starting job when the senior ahead of him blew off practice. Waller's high school coach didn't know how lucky he was. Waller would go on to set state scoring records and be named Delaware's athlete of the year in 1950. After an All-American career at Maryland, he was a first-round pick of the Los Angeles Rams; he finished second in Rookie of the Year voting after his first season and made the Pro Bowl.

If not for injuries, who knows how great his career could have been. But after just four seasons he was forced to retire and go into coaching. The year before being named head coach of the Bell, Ron spent half a season as the interim coach for the San Diego Chargers, going 1–5.

Waller and Corcoran would be our leaders, and no one dared criticize their credentials. Regardless of their records or stats, they had played and coached at professional football's highest levels. We were just a bunch of sandlot scrubs looking to prolong a dream.

Before beginning the practice, Ron assembled us for a speech. He explained what the Bell was, when we'd be playing, and that he didn't know if anyone here was worth his time, but hoped someone would show him something. If he got lucky and someone did, they'd be invited to a second try-out. Then he broke us down into groups by position.

As they checked us in the coaches asked us our names, ages, and organized football experience. I was twenty-eight years old and had played just one year of high school football and one year of semi-pro. No one was going to be impressed that I was the best receiver Max's Tavern of the DelCo rough touch league had ever had. So I lied. I told the receivers' coach I was twenty-four and had played college football at Villanova. Hey, I had nothing to lose.

The first thing they had us do was run the forty-yard dash, which is the barometer by which everything speed-related is measured in football. Coaches drool when they see someone run a fast forty, which in those days was anything under 4.6 seconds. As every player has gotten bigger, faster, and stronger, there's even more of a premium placed on speed today. Players without any skill at all are drafted and given millions of dollars if they can run fast. Tackling can be taught. Catching can be taught. But, as the coaching axiom goes, speed can't be taught.

It was like the Aston Knights tryout all over again. The first thing I was being asked to do was run fast. How could I not make this team? I watched a lot of the guys go before me and I was thinking I was golden. While waiting my turn I stepped away from the other potential players and did something I used to do as a pole-vaulter—visualization. I imagined myself as a cheetah, running gracefully in slow motion. I saw myself relaxing my jaw, touching my index finger to my thumb, moving my arms back and forth so my upper body didn't lock up. All of the things that Marty Stern taught me about sprinting in eighth grade were running through my head. When my turn came, I heard the gun and I drove my legs as hard as I could, taking long, graceful strides across the grass. When I crossed the finish line I heard the timer yell, "Four point five." I was elated. No one had run that fast. I thought I was in.

The position coaches hadn't been monitoring the forty times because they'd been working with some of the players who had already been signed. Instead, their assistants kept the time and let their bosses know who was the fastest. Then the position coaches came over and called out the names of fifteen guys they wanted to move to the agility station on the field. Everyone else was told thanks for coming by. Only my name wasn't on the list. Suddenly it was the Drake and Penn Relays all over again. I was being shut out for reasons I didn't know. Unlike the decathlon, I couldn't let this opportunity pass. For once I stood up for myself. I yelled out, "What is the criteria?" The coach, who had begun to walk away, turned around and shot me a look. He couldn't believe I was challenging him.

"We're taking the fastest forty times," he said.

"I ran a four five, that was the fastest forty time here," I said.

"Yeah, but I've never seen a white guy run that fast. My assistant must have timed you wrong," he said to me.

"Give me another chance," I said, stepping forward.

He just shrugged, indicating he didn't want to be bothered but knew fighting with me would take longer than the time it took me to run again. So they lined me up, with four guys timing me this time. It was in the morning, on wet grass. And when they said go, I came flying off the line. I had a beautiful, full stride, with my arms and legs pumping like pistons. It was just powerful. I crossed the line in 4.5 seconds, again. And this time the coach knew I was legit. He told me to go on to the agility drills.

Now I was rolling. We did one-on-one matchups, and I knew there wasn't a defensive back that could run with me. Then we did seven-on-seven drills, which was no different to me from playing rough touch on Sunday mornings. After lunch break and a chalk talk where they drew up plays for us to run, there were only about forty of us remaining out of the six hundred who showed up for tryouts. I had always had an inate ability to read defenses, and I showed it that afternoon.

That's when Ron Waller told me I'd been invited to a second tryout.

This one was at JFK Stadium, where the Bell was going to play its home games. It was a massive, rickety, old, horseshoe-shaped stadium built in the early 1920s. It was in such bad shape that, from 1958 until 1970, the Eagles chose to share a home stadium with the University of Pennsylvania rather than play at JFK. As I jogged around the track that surrounded the field I saw a familiar face. It was Johnny Bosacco, whose brothers had coached one of my Pee Wee football teams more than twenty years earlier. I ran over to chat him up and asked, "What are you doing here?"

"I own the team," he said. "What are you doing here?"

"I'm trying out."

Having the team owner on my side didn't hurt my chances. And even after I fessed up about my real age and lack of college football experience, I needed only another good performance during that tryout to get an invite to training camp. Even before training camp began that June, they asked me to sign a contract. So, on May 5, 1974, I officially became a professional football player. If I made the team, I'd be paid $16,000 for six months' work, which was $4,000 more than I was making as a teacher at Interboro.

I had a month to get in shape for camp. Waller had given all the invitees a training regiment he expected us to follow before practice started. It was hours a day of conditioning drills: running backward; running stadium steps; practicing hip rolls and our lateral movement; doing thousands of up downs, which is when you run in place, drop to the ground, and then bounce back up. This was more than I could do in a couple hours before school or a couple hours after. It was a full-time job.

I had been teaching and coaching in the Interboro school system for six years now. I was popular with students, my teams won, and I was getting my master's degree in counseling. No one could doubt my dedication to the school or the kids or my job. I had a lot of goodwill on my side. Which is why, when I asked the superintendent of schools for a temporary leave over the last month of the school year, he didn't hesitate to say yes. If I didn't make the Bell, I could have my job again the next fall. But if I did, well, I'm not sure either one of us considered what would happen then.

My last day of school was the Monday after I signed my contract. I drove up in my 1972 Mercury Cougar, painted yellow with a black top. I had long hair, and was wearing white pants and a white shirt with powder-blue flowers on it and a collar that spread out to my shoulders. I thought I was one cool dude. I felt more excited about the opportunity than melancholy about what I was leaving behind. At least until my second-period class. I had become especially close with a lot of the students in the class. And at the end of the period, one of them pulled out a Chicago album, put it on a record player I had in the classroom, and played the song "Colour My World." It was a love song, but the opening line is what they wanted to convey: "As time goes on, I realize just what you mean to me." Ten years earlier it would have seemed inappropriate. But it was the early seventies now, counterculture was king, and kids were all about communicating their feelings as relationships between teachers and students were less formal. I didn't intimidate or bully my kids, and they didn't see me as someone they had to hide things from. They appreciated it, and this was their way of showing me.

Besides, even if I wasn't in the classroom, I was still teaching them something. I was twenty-eight years old and chasing a dream. There was a lesson in that that would stick with them forever.

The Bell was going to bring more than one hundred players to camp. Even in a start-up league, on a team whose highest profile players were washed out pros and guys who lit up the Seaboard League, I was a long shot to make it. But I wanted it. Badly. So badly I did nothing for the next four weeks but train. I ran the steps at Interboro's football stadium so often I could feel my knees involuntarily climbing as I drifted off to sleep. I did up downs until I couldn't count how many I had done. I ran backward nearly as fast as I could run forward.

I'd exercise in the morning with a former student named Chubby Price, who was getting in shape to become a tennis pro. He was a quarterback in high school and in the afternoons he'd throw me passes so I could work on my hands. Then I'd help him with agility and quickness drills. That lasted for a week before I got a call from Ron Holliday, who was a couple years younger than me and grew up in Berwyn, just outside of Philadelphia. Ron spent the 1973 season as a little-used receiver for Waller on the Chargers. After that year with San Diego Ron signed with Waller and the Bell. He was one of the guys clocking times at that first tryout. And maybe he saw something in me that he thought he could help develop. Or he just needed someone local to work out with. That's how little people expected of me. My own competition at wide receiver was calling me to help keep him in shape.

But I think I got more out of it than he did. I didn't know how to play wide receiver at the professional level. I was completely unpolished. And Ron gave me pointers. He invited me to work out with him and other NFL players at Franklin field. When I ran pass routes I turned my shoulders in the direction I was headed, giving away where the pass would be. So I worked on keeping my shoulders square. He taught me how to work back to the ball instead of waiting for it to come to me. There were probably a hundred little things like that, things that separate guys of equal talent, which, when done, turn some into All-Pros and others into nothing more than season-ticket holders. I had to learn to do all of them, every time, if I was going to make it.

I was so focused on training I never thought about what would happen next: How would I do at training camp? What if I made the team? What if I didn't? I was dedicated to being in shape and not embarrassing myself in the first few days of camp. Then, as soon as I weighed the possibilities, for both success and failure, doubts started creeping in. I had something to lose. Ever since I had been rejected by the Penn and Drake Relays, I had felt like my athletic career was incomplete, my potential unfulfilled. I needed to prove to myself, to Janet, to the relay organizers, to the guys in rough touch and Johnny Moran and the players in the Eastern Seaboard League. I needed to show them all that I was a real athlete, not just a weekend warrior who peaked in college.

That first night of training camp was bad. We were practicing at Glassboro State Teachers College. I was sharing a room with a young kid just out of college who had never had a job. I lay in bed that night, listening to him snore, nervous as a cat in a room full of rocking chairs. I was thinking, What am I doing here? If I made it I would have to quit a job that I love, where I was comfortable and secure. I'd be venturing out into the real world as an adult for the first time. I realized I was knocking on the door of professional football, and I wasn't sure I wanted to walk through.

I started feeling better once practices began. For the first time in my life I was playing against a full defense of players who had played in the NFL and in college. They tried to rough me up and intimidate me, and they were on my team. The practices were brutal—close to three hours long in the sun. But Waller always dressed the same, no matter how hot it was. He wore a thin, green rubber shirt that was cinched up at his neck, the kind of shirts wrestlers wore in the days before a match, when they were trying to lose weight by sweating. It was so tight at his neck, and always so hot outside, his face was constantly a bright red. Then he kept his white socks pulled all the way up to his knees.

Despite the conditions, I held my own. In scrimmages I

would blindside guys and throw cross-body blocks. I made some nice catches—even though I still hadn't mastered everything Holliday tried to teach me—and was a quick study in the film room. More than anything, I just wanted to sprint past somebody. Then came our preseason game against the New York Stars. The play call was a run, a sweep to my side, with the entire offensive line pulling toward me and creating a wall of blockers in front of the running back. My job was to take out the linebacker in pursuit. And did I. As he sprinted toward the runner he was so zeroed in he didn't see me coming. I hit him full on in the solar plexus, laying him out on his back. But I never left my feet. And as I looked back to see where the runner was I noticed he was just passing me and racing down the sideline, with one defender to beat. I took off at a full gallop and, at the five-yard line, wiped out the lone defender, as our back waltzed into the end zone untouched.

The next day Ron Waller approached me in the crowded locker room after practice. He quieted everyone down and said, "Look at this, guys. Look at this. This old man has made the team."

My professional football career had begun.

SEVEN

THE WORLD Football League was the brainchild of Gary Davidson, a Southern California tax lawyer turned entrepreneur who made it his mission to tweak professional sports leagues. In 1967, when he was just thirty-three, he and a partner formed the American Basketball Association (ABA) to compete with the National Basketball Association. In 1972, he started the World Hockey Association (WHA) to take on the National Hockey League. He was a charming, smooth-talking, blond-haired man who easily convinced multi-millionaires that the best way to play with their money was to buy into professional sports. This was before free agency had turned every pro athlete into a millionaire, and Davidson saw an opportunity to lure the biggest stars in sports to new leagues with his huge dollars. He signed Gordie Howe and Bobby Hull to the WHA. In 1971, he gave Julius Erving, at the time the best college basketball player in the country, $500,000 to leave school early and sign with the Virginia Squires in the ABA. This was at a time when only a handful of NBA players were making six figures in a season. After Davidson's dealings, however, the average salary in the NBA quadrupled. Eventually, the NBA was forced to absorb some teams from the ABA. Same with the NHL and WHA.

Davidson's strategy with the WFL was no different: Dole out huge amounts of cash, make splashy signings, and watch the NFL quake because of the upstart. The league's first big deals were with three Miami Dolphins stars: running backs Larry Csonka and Jim Kiick and receiver Paul Warfield. They signed for a combined $3.5 million to play for the Toronto Northmen beginning in 1975. At the time, it was one of the biggest deals ever in sports. Even if the league folded before the 1975 season, their contracts were guaranteed. A game hadn't been played yet, but the league had announced its presence.

My signing, however, made a little less news. There was a story in the *Delaware County Daily Times* in which one of the writers visited with me during my last day at school. And when I made the team, the *Jolly Roger,* the official school paper of Interboro Junior High wrote, under the headline "Bell Wins, Interboro Loses," that "Mr. Papale sorrowfully leaves our hallowed halls. This person has done much for us, giving his time and effort to uplift school spirit. Mr. Papale has CARED about the school and its students and we thank him."

That was actually the most encouragement the Bell got early

on. While so many WFL franchises threw money around to make big-name signings, the Bell was more frugal. The team signed Tim Rossovich, who had been an All-Pro linebacker for the Eagles in 1969. But he was actually better known for his off-field stunts, which included eating glass beer mugs for fun and lighting his wildly untamed curly hair on fire as a party trick. It's no wonder that, after his NFL career was over, Rossovich moved to Hollywood and became an actor. Even with a crazy man like Rossovich we were basically the Pottstown Firebirds of the Seaboard League, with some other not-so-big names thrown into the mix. Our leading scorer that year was running back John Laud. His blocking back was Claude Watts, who had been playing semi-pro for so long no one knew how old he was. He could have been thirty-five. He could have been fifty. Claude didn't even pick up his feet when he ran, he just shuffled them along, shedding tacklers as if he were a bulldozer.

The weeks leading up to the season were particularly tough. Practices were long, especially for wide receivers. Waller loved a passing offense, which meant we were sprinting for nearly all three hours we were on the field. Shortly before the season began we moved our practices from Glassboro State to JFK stadium. The locker room looked like it hadn't been upgraded since the stadium opened fifty years earlier. It was actually on the second level of the stadium, and we had to walk up a set of rickety, rusty steps to get to it. Inside, there were rats being chased by cats. Any minute we expected dogs to come in after the cats, and we worried who might be coming to take care of us. At the end of the day you wanted to hear or read something positive about your efforts, but the media in Philly thought we were a joke. The most popular broadcaster in town was "Big" Al Meltzer. He was close to six-five and was a fixture in Philadelphia. He would go on the air and editorialize that the league was inferior and it was wasting the time of fans and the journalists who had to cover it.

There was nothing traditional about the league, which is one reason it was judged so harshly before we ever played a game. With the ABA and the WHA, Davidson took everything he didn't like about pro basketball and hockey and got rid of it. The ABA ball was red, white, and blue. The WHA puck was dark blue. He invented the slam-dunk contest. In the WFL, the ball was blue and gold. Goal posts were put in the back of the end zone, instead of at the goal line like in the NFL. The season was twenty games long, lasting from July until November. Of course, in 1974, two months after the WFL had its first game, the NFL moved its goal posts to the back of the end zone. And, by the 1978 season, it increased the amount of games each of its teams played from fourteen to sixteen.

Because of the bad press and our lack of a high-profile star, we didn't expect to get much fan support for our first game, on July 10, 1974. JFK stadium held one hundred thousand people, and we assumed anyone who showed up would have their pick of seats. But just as our season began there were reports that NFL players would go on strike before training camp started that summer. And, as we dressed in our mustard-yellow and blue uniforms before our first game, we could hear a low rumble outside our locker room. People were actually filling the stadium. When we ran through the tunnel and onto the track surrounding the field, there was a loud roar. For us. We had fans cheering for us. People were leaning over the railing just outside of our tunnel entrance asking us for autographs. A lot of them were cheering for me. I was announced as a starting wide receiver, number 83, in front of my mom, dad, sister, and seemingly half of Delaware County.

We were playing the Portland Storm, who was, as Waller understated before the game, "an unknown quantity." The biggest name in their training camp had been Dino Martin, Dean Martin's son, a former tennis player at USC who, six months earlier, had been arrested for possession of seven machine guns and an anti-tank gun. The Storm hadn't played any scrimmages during training camp, so the first time they lined up as a team was against us. And it showed. We had been going twice a day for thirty days and then running a mile after practice. We were anxious to get out there, and Waller couldn't wait to run some new plays he designed. He had us lining up in formations that looked like figure eights. We had three backs lined up behind the quarterback. Or receivers lined up behind one another on each side of the line. The Portland defenders literally couldn't find guys to cover.

Our game was the first one played in the World Football League. And on our opening drive I ran a quick out, our first pass play, and King Corcoran hit me for a short gain. I made the first ever reception in WFL history. I didn't get any calls from the Hall of Fame asking for my jersey to honor the significance of the catch. But hey, it wasn't bad for an old man who played only one year of high school football. We'd go on to beat the Storm easily, 33–8. After the game, as I walked through our end zone toward the tunnel that led to our locker room, I saw close to fifty kids running toward me. It was a group of my students from Interboro, who mobbed me in the end zone. We were all euphoric: my students, the fans, my teammates, and me. And it clearly made some of us a little too giddy, as Corcoran boasted to a reporter from the *Philadelphia Inquirer*, "I think we could stay with New England and Houston of the NFL and guys like that."

Corcoran was a pretty confident guy. He liked to wear white shoes and a white cap and he carried himself like he believed he was a pro, no matter what the score of the game. He had the kind of confidence that made him comfortable taking some time out of practice on real sunny days to sit in the stands at JFK, tilt his head back, lay a reflector on his chest, and get himself a tan. But I was caught up in the hoopla, too, setting up an appearance at a Glenolden barbershop to sign autographs. I even called the Bell to get them to send over some photos of me in my uniform. Our marketing director was a young kid named Dick Pollak, who had been promoted from intern. He thought personal appearances were such a good idea that he soon had me doing them all over the city. But the reality was that we wouldn't play as well as we did that first game for the rest of the season. We lost our next two games before heading out to Portland for a rematch with the Storm. We got back in the win column, but, by then, the league had become the laughingstock everyone expected it to be.

The attendance league-wide for the first weekend of games averaged more than forty-three thousand fans, which was higher than what the AFL did in its opening weekend. But then the Jacksonville Sharks admitted that they gave away forty-four thousand tickets to their home opener. We averaged sixty thousand our first two games, although almost no one paid the $76 it cost for a nine-game, season-ticket package. Nearly one hundred thousand tickets were given away those first two weekends. We started calling them the Domino sugar games, because Domino ran a promotion that gave anyone who bought a bag of Domino sugar a free ticket to a Bell game. By September, less than two months after games began, the New York franchise relocated to Charlotte and the Houston team moved to Shreveport. In October, the teams in Jacksonville and Detroit just went out of business without bothering to move. There were rumors that players in Portland were being fed by locals and that the Charlotte team, shortly after moving from New York, had its uniforms impounded because the New York owners hadn't paid the laundry bill. We once waited at our hotel in Anaheim for our luxury coaches to arrive and take us to a game. They never appeared, so we called a busing company that sent over these school buses that carried migrant workers to jobs all over Southern California. All of us had long hair, wore T-shirts, and didn't look like professional players. When we got to the stadium, it took twenty minutes to convince security we were actually the team and not workers trying to sneak in to a WFL game.

Still, you wouldn't think we were bush league watching Ron Waller. He was as intense as any coach I had ever had up to that point. One game, after I had played nearly every play of the first half on offense and on special teams, I ran a route incorrectly in overtime. It was ninety-five degrees on the field and players were passing out. Waller pulled me off the field and told me I was fined $25. Waller was an offense-minded coach, and he had the most elaborate schemes in which just about every receiver was open at one time or another during the play, but Corcoran rarely seemed to be looking my way.

While I started those first few games at wide receiver, I hadn't made many catches. Three the first game, and just a couple in the two games after that. But against the Storm in Portland, early in the game, Corcoran found me on a quick slant running across the middle. This is one of the most dangerous plays in football. The pattern takes the receiver through the middle of the defense and forces him to turn his back toward the linebackers or defensive backs who are just waiting to tee off on him. I wasn't going to complain about going over the middle, but it wasn't my favorite play in the playbook. As soon as I caught Corcoran's pass a defensive back nailed me. He had been watching the quarterback the whole time, read the play, knew exactly where the ball was going, and got a running start to time his hit perfectly. Not only did I not hold on to the ball, I didn't even stay conscious.

I don't know how long I was laid out on the field, but when I woke up I didn't see a doctor or trainer standing next to me. I saw Corcoran. He was yelling at me because I had dropped the ball.

After the game was over, and we were in the locker room, with strips of smelling salts still stuck up my nose, I laced into him. I let him know what I thought of him and his quarterbacking in less than polite terms. Then Waller deactivated me for the next three games.

When I returned at the end of August I had been demoted from wide receiver to tight end. Now my job was almost exclusively about making crack blocks, opening holes for our running backs, and catching a pass if a blitzer was chasing Corcoran. In Waller's wide-open offenses, there wasn't much use for a tight end. Not that I was in it to lead the league in receptions. I never lost perspective. I was a twenty-eight-year-old rookie in professional football. If all I did was play special teams during practice I wouldn't have cared. My lack of stats didn't keep friends and family from coming to the games, either. As the crowds dwindled, it became easier to spot my mom, dad, and sister in the stands. They were always there, every home game. There was a difference in the support my father, most of all, gave me as a pro compared to when I was growing up. Back then he never cheered, only criticized. But now I felt as though I could hear him chanting my name above all the other voices. He was so clearly proud of me; there was never any criticism anymore, only compliments. Me making it, even in the WFL, had felt to him as though he had made it, and it seemed to make the rest of his life easier, or at least more bearable.

But at the end of August, my first game back from my suspension, we all suffered a setback. I trotted out onto the field and scanned the almost empty stands looking for my family. After kickoff, they still weren't there. As the game dragged on, they never showed up. My father hadn't missed one of my games or meets in all these years. Meanwhile, my sister and my mom, especially, loved getting out of the house. My mom didn't ride the officials like she had when I was in junior high, but she enjoyed the atmosphere. If none of them were there, then something was wrong. Back in the locker room after the game Waller called me into his office. He told me my mom was very sick. It didn't occur to me at the time to ask how he knew. (I would find out later that Bell officials heard from the hospital before the game began but waited until after it was over to tell me.) I raced out of the stadium and found my dad and sister huddling over my mom's hospital bed. A priest had been there to give her last rites; they didn't expect her to last the night. And I nearly missed it. I sat by her bedside all through the night as she slowly fought her way back to life.

I rejoined the team the next week, but my heart wasn't entirely in it. I was angry the Bell had withheld information about my mom's illness. If she had died I wouldn't have been there. Plus, I was playing out of position at tight end. And we weren't very good. When I suffered another concussion in mid-October there were just four games left in the year. Ron Waller told me my season was over. He moved me up to the broadcast booth to help the announcers. And I didn't argue with him.

EVEN WITH ALL the problems—for me, the team, the league—I had no doubts I was coming back the next year. I had no doubts the WFL would succeed and I would be a professional football player for as long as I wanted. I spent weekdays during the off-season substitute teaching at Interboro and weekends tending bar at the Mariner's Gallery Inn in a little town called Aston, ten miles from where I lived. Every once in a while, I would take an afternoon behind the bar, too, just to make some extra cash. Because, while I had no doubt I'd make the team in 1975, I wasn't going to get rich playing football.

Before the season began the Bell signed a former Penn State superstar named Ted Kwalick. Kwalick had been a two-time All-American tight end with the Nittany Lions and then a three-time Pro Bowler with the San Francisco 49ers. He was the first NFL player the Bell lured to the league who was in his prime, and because he was a local product, management expected attendance to skyrocket. Since I was a veteran, they wanted to give me a piece of the riches. So, instead of signing me to a raise on the $16,000 I had made as a rookie in 1974, they offered me $14,000 and a percentage of the gate receipts. It seemed like a deal I couldn't refuse, mainly because I wasn't given a choice.

Of course, as soon as I got a letter from Ron Waller that

began "Dear Veteran," all was forgiven. I was a veteran on my way to my second training camp. I couldn't really complain about that. With Kwalick and a new quarterback—we had signed Joe Namath's backup Bob Davis—our offense would look close to professional.

But Waller wouldn't be around to coach it. Before we got to training camp, he was fired, and replaced by Willie Wood, the ex-Packer Hall of Fame defensive back. When he was hired, Wood became the first black head coach in professional football history.

Wood had originally been hired to be our defensive coordinator, and he didn't care too much about offense. That first month of the season we didn't light up the scoreboard, averaging fewer than twenty points a game. While I did what I could early on, catching a forty-nine-yard touchdown pass, it was pretty clear that my role was going to be on special teams, sprinting down the field as fast as I could and throwing my body into the other team's first line of blockers.

Special teams was how I made the biggest impression during my time with the Bell. That's where the hardest workers and biggest underdogs on every football team play and the Bell fans, however few there were, were mostly South Philly, blue-collar Italian guys who rooted for the scrappiest players. In my first season the special-teams coach, Joe Gardi, used to beg Waller to let the special-teams guys be introduced. Before every game, either the starting offense or defense is usually introduced. But Waller didn't care about that stuff, so whenever Gardi asked he said sure. For most home games, I was the one leading the team onto the field, my long hair peeking out from underneath my helmet.

Early in the season, it was special teams that got me noticed by Wood, too. I had nearly dislocated my elbow earlier in a game but didn't want to come out. Then, while setting up for a punt return, I was lined up on the outside to block the opponent's fastest guy. His sole purpose was to get downfield and make that first hit on the return man. Normally, the guys outside on special teams engage in a few seconds of hand-to-hand combat. But, when he came at me at the snap, I went low and cut him down. We got up again, but I got up faster—thank God for the millions of up downs Waller used to make us do—and I cut him down again. And then again. And then again. Four times he tried getting by me and I cut blocked him every time. It was all I could do since I couldn't engage him with my injured elbow. Wood loved that I did that. And he made sure my teammates saw it in the film room.

The team had a great chemistry under Wood and his assistants, including Hall of Famers Herb Adderley and Leroy Kelly and an ex-Eagle, Bobby Pelligrini, who played on the title team in 1960. He was respected because of what he had done in the NFL. He treated us like pros, no matter how badly the league was doing financially or the team was doing on the field or the ridiculous levels we stooped to for attention. Before the first exhibition game we were told that every position was going to wear a different color pair of pants, so fans could identify us better. But we didn't get the standard blue, green, orange, or red. Some players had bright pink with black stripes, others had yellow with black stripes or green. The quarterback wore white pants with brightly colored stars on them. But, amazingly, even the pastel-colored pants didn't draw fans in. By mid-season our attendance was sagging and our superstar draw, Kwalick, wasn't even leading the team in receptions. But we liked one another and hung out off the field, especially Bobby Davis and me. He had great stories about playing with Namath, which I loved hearing. And since we were nearly the same age and liked to hit the town, it was natural we got together.

One night we went to a club called Green Streets on Walnut in the center of Philly. It had a restaurant, private rooms, a huge dance floor, and a lounge that felt like it could fit half of Philadelphia. It was owned by Stanley Green, a nightclub fixture in Philly. Every Wednesday at Green Streets was secretaries' night, and Stanley tried to get celebrities in to increase the draw. It was a little more than a week before Halloween, and on this night members of the Bell had been asked to attend. Bobby and I showed up early so we could get a good seat at the bar. We were hanging out, and the bartender recognized Bobby and started chatting us up. As we were talking there was a radio playing in the background. Then, during a break in the music, Bobby and I both heard this announcement: "The WFL has folded." We looked at each other, both wondering if the other had heard it, hoping we had been mistaken. The looks on our faces made it clear we weren't hearing things, so Bobby asked the bartender to turn on the TV.

It was around six o'clock and the news was on, which meant we had to wait for the sports. It was excruciating. But when it finally happened, when the sportscaster showed footage of a news conference from earlier that afternoon in which the WFL commissioner was announcing the league had gone under, we were shocked. Everything the commissioner said made sense: Attendance was waning, teams were going under, and the league was $20 million in debt and didn't have the cash to keep it going. But we didn't want to believe it. We had just been at practice that afternoon and no one had mentioned anything to us.

This was before the age of cell phones, so Bobby stood up and went to a pay phone to call his agent. When he came back to the bar more of our teammates were there. Some of them hadn't heard the news. By the end of the night, most of the team was lined up at the bar, ordering drinks and talking about one and a half seasons worth of memories. Secretaries' night at Green Streets turned out to be our going-away party.

The next day Bobby and I drove over to the stadium together to clean out our lockers, but when we got to one of the gates it was locked. They all were. We had no way in. Whatever was in our lockers was gone forever. Just like the league.

I DIDN'T SEE myself as a failure. I had chased a dream and caught it. It didn't matter to me that it hadn't been the NFL. It was closer than most people would ever get. I had closed that circle and felt I had reached my fullest potential as an athlete. Come the following fall, I would go back to teaching full-time, finish my master's, and have no regrets. Until then I planned to substitute teach at Interboro and bartend at the Mariner's Gallery Inn. I had an apartment in a fancy complex called Ramblewood and a new car and there was more debt than there was income, so I bartended as much as I could.

But, in the back of my mind, I wondered if the Eagles had noticed me. The day the league folded they signed two of our offensive linemen, John Roman and Don Ratliff. And even as their season ended, I held out hope. Rich Iannarella, the Bell's general manager, kept whispering in my ear that I could play in the NFL. He said he was good friends with the Eagles' GM, Jim Murray, and would recommend that the Eagles give me a look. As usual, the Eagles were really bad. Every year after their 1960 championship season they seemed to get worse, as they went through six coaches in fourteen years and had just two winning records between 1961 and 1975. In 1975 they finished 4–10, the ninth straight year they finished .500 or worse and fired their coach yet again. Signing a special-teams standout from the WFL wouldn't make them any worse.

I didn't wait by the phone. I had bills to pay and even pulling extra hours at the bar wasn't helping me cover them. On weekends I hung out at a place called Fran O'Brien's, which was a supper club on City Line Avenue on the Main Line. I'd usually go decked out. One of the bouncers there happened to be Denny Franks, a former All-American center at Michigan who had spent the previous summer in the Eagles training camp before getting cut. He played a couple weeks with the Raiders during the 1975 season and was cut from there, too. So he moved back to Philly and spent the rest of the winter and the next spring in town, hoping to catch on with the Eagles in 1976. In the meantime, he was working the door at Fran O'Brien's and he hated seeing me coming. He was six-two and thick and he thought I was just some kind of pretty boy. One night in the bar I happened to be talking to the owner and mentioned that I needed to find extra work. He offered to make me a bouncer on the weekends, working right next to Denny. I didn't hesitate to say yes. That was an extra $100 a night in my pocket, guaranteed, plus the five bucks people waiting in line would slip me just to get through the door.

Denny would barely talk to me when we worked. We'd just stand there, both looking sharp in three-piece suits. Then, one night, we were called inside to settle down one of the customers who was creating a disturbance. He was in a booth with about ten of his friends. When we walked over he reached into his jacket pocket. Someone yelled, "He's got a gun." Before Denny or I could grab him we were surrounded by his ten buddies. The owner walked over and tried to calm things down. But we knew that wouldn't last long. He wore glasses, and the surest sign he was ready to pop somebody was when he took off his glasses, rubbed his nose, and said, "I don't want anyone here to get hurt." Then he'd slug someone right in the face.

Denny and I were back-to-back, like Butch and Sundance when they were circled by the bad guys. Those guys then beat the pulp out of us, and their girlfriends were hitting us over the heads with purses. Our three-piece suits were cut into shreds. But after that, Denny and I became the closest of friends. We called ourselves Fran O'Brien's floor control engineers and developed a real nice rapport. We were both party-hard, play-hard, and go-all-out kinds of guys.

One night working the door we noticed these two gorgeous women standing at the end of the line waiting to get in. Denny walked back to them and said, "Ladies, your reservation is ready." They laughed, knowing they didn't have a reservation, but played along. They were sisters, Sandy and Jackie Bianchini, and Denny and I spent most of what we made that night buying them drinks once we were off duty. Sandy must have appreciated that, because shortly after we started dating.

Despite the fact we had developed this great friendship, Denny couldn't help but laugh the first time I told him I wanted to get a tryout with the Eagles. To him I probably sounded like an idiot. He had played in the Rose Bowl and been a great college player, but had gone through the wringer trying to make it in the league during the previous year. He saw me as some naïve local kid who figured if I could make it in the WFL, I could make it in the NFL. He asked me if I was sure I wasn't worried about messing up my face. Then he asked where I had gone to school. When I said St. Joe's he asked me what position I played. I don't think the words "I didn't play in college" were out of my mouth before he started laughing at me. He just said, "Boy, you are one loooooooong shot."

I had been working out regularly since the WFL season ended, and Rich Iannarella, who had become my agent, kept telling me something was going to happen with an NFL team come training camp. He said the Jets and the Eagles were interested in me. But I didn't believe him. That February the Eagles had hired a thirty-nine-year-old coaching prodigy named Dick Vermeil, who had just coached UCLA to a Rose Bowl upset of number-one-ranked Ohio State. New coaches don't offer jobs to thirty-year-old rookies. Not if they expect to stay NFL coaches for very long.

As winter turned to spring, I started getting anxious. Richie had told me the Eagles were having a two-day tryout beginning April 24. I knew better than to get my hopes up, but every time the phone rang I practically jumped out of my chair. Finally, on April 20, 1976, I got the call. "The Eagles want you to report to the Vet for camp this weekend," Richie said.

In 1971 the Eagles left Franklin Field for Veterans Stadium. At the time it was a state-of-the-art, $65-million facility. At least that's how it was billed. But when players arrived for their first preseason game ever at the stadium, they immediately realized that the locker room didn't have air-conditioning. It was so hot inside the cramped room that players had to get dressed in the corridor. While the AC was fixed, there were bigger problems that would never be taken care of. The night before that first preseason game, one Eagles executive walked along the field and, when he stepped on the fifteen-yard line, the lower half of his leg disappeared into a deep hole. Over the next thirty years, the field conditions would never improve. It was like playing on concrete covered by a very thin layer of carpet. In some cases there was nothing but wood underneath the Astroturf. One NFL player's career ended when he blew out both of his knees on the same play. Around the league, players usually feared playing at the Vet because of the field a lot more than because of the Eagles. In 2001, the field was in such bad shape a game was actually canceled.

But, to me, the Vet was like the Taj Mahal. My new seats were in the 700-level, where the meanest of the notorious ornery Eagles fans settled. How tough are they? Hall of Fame quarterback Sonny Jurgensen began his career with the Eagles in 1957. He won three of his first four starts, and when he went into the tunnel toward the locker room after one of those wins fans threw beer cans at him.

Philly is a blue-collar city, and football is a tough, blue-collar game. If we didn't see effort on the field that was equal to what we gave at our jobs during the week, we got pretty mad. But all the bile Eagles fans spew comes from their passion for the team. The team didn't stop selling out the stadium in the sixties and seventies, when two-win seasons were the norm. Even if fans were coming out just to boo, they were still coming out. I was one of them.

Which is why, when I walked into the locker room at the Vet to get dressed for that first tryout, I felt as though I were worshipping in the temple of my religion for the first time. It was nearly empty, just a couple other guys getting dressed or warming up. They were my competition, but I didn't even notice them. I saw the nameplates of the players I had been cheering for. There was the locker of Roman Gabriel, the Eagles quarterback. And Harold Carmichael's, their six-eight wide receiver, and Bill Bergey's, their All-Pro middle linebacker who was so intimidating even the nastiest fans in the 700-level were afraid to boo him. I had been given a set of shoulder pads, a practice jersey, and a helmet, all three of which were sitting at my feet as I spun around the room, soaking it all in. I must have stood there for twenty minutes, as the rest of the potential players came in, stretched, got dressed, and walked out to the field. The memories from a lifetime of cheering for, and escaping with, the Eagles were playing in my head. I saw myself pretending to be Tommy McDonald in my backyard. I saw Chuck Bednarik sitting on Jim Taylor in 1960. I saw me and Chuck Gardner and Billy Thomas snaking through the crowd to get to our seats at Franklin Field. I had completely forgotten why I was there. Then I turned around and realized I was alone, still not dressed and late for the tryout.

I threw on my pads, my jersey, and my helmet and sprinted out of the locker room. But I had no idea how to get out of the stadium. We were practicing at JFK, which was across the street from the Vet, and I ran left, down a long concrete corridor that seemed to have no end. I heard my cleats echoing through the hall and started to sweat because I couldn't find my way out. I ran for five or six minutes, as hard as I could, and there were no obvious exits. My pads were starting to get heavy and I worried what it would look like if someone saw me, running around with my helmet on, panting and screaming, "Get me out of here." Finally someone heard me, didn't run away, and showed me the way out.

I ran across the parking lot, my cleats sounding like tap shoes on the concrete, and found the tunnel to JFK. I didn't even think about trying to sneak into practice. I ran out of the tunnel in a full sprint, so fast it was impossible to be ignored. The rest of the players were stretching in the middle of the field. Vermeil just looked at me. No, actually, he looked through me with what my future Eagle teammates and I would affectionately call "The Hairy Eyeball." It was as though he were vaporizing me right there on the field. I walked past him, figuring if he didn't kick me out I was just going to join the other guys as they stretched. As soon as I took a seat and began to loosen up I heard a voice from the stands. "Here we go, Vincie." It was my dad. He had come to the tryout to cheer me on. And the only thing at that moment that upset me more than being on the wrong end of Vermeil's stare was the idea of letting down my father. Even as an adult I still felt that way, only now it was because I knew how much it meant to him, not because of how he'd treat me if I failed.

Vermeil had us run the forty, which I ran as well as I did at the WFL tryouts. We went through agility drills. We ran routes one-on-one and seven-on-seven. That's when I knew I could make this team. I blew by defenders, found open spots in the defense, and came out of my breaks in control and able to catch the ball. I had an advantage playing at JFK. I knew the dips in the field from my days with the Bell. I still wasn't a completely polished receiver, but for an open tryout, I was awfully good. When it was over Vermeil pulled me aside. I had heard he was a real disciplinarian and I expected him to tell me that he appreciated my coming out, but because I came in late and disrupted practice, he wouldn't be needing me. Instead, he told me he liked what I could do. "Especially," he said, "the way you run."

The entire practice was filmed. And after what must have been a week of studying all the attendees, the Eagles offered me a contract. I had been invited to training camp. If I made the team I'd be paid $21,000 and a $3,000 bonus. But there were no guarantees I'd make it.

Now I had to get ready.

EIGHT

WANTED TO report to that training camp in the best shape of my life. If I was cut I at least wanted to know that I'd done my best. I didn't want to show up in mediocre condition and spend the rest of my days asking myself, Gee, if only I worked a little harder, would I have made it?

I didn't need to look far for inspiration. I looked at my father still working the line at Westinghouse and told myself I had it easy. As soon as I signed the deal at the end of April I made the Vet my second home. Denny Franks and I worked out together. I helped him learn how to run and improve his speed. He taught me how to lift weights, which I had never done in my life. We both worked with the Eagles' assistant trainer, Ron O'Neal, and the strength and conditioning coach, Gus Hoefling, who taught us martial arts. By the time camp arrived I felt like a machine. I was six-two, 195 pounds, and, even at thirty, knew I was still as fast as anyone the Eagles had on their team.

We opened training camp at Widener College on July 3. Almost immediately I was confronted with a challenge. A sign over the double-glass doors at the entrance to the dorm read AUTHORIZED PERSONNEL ONLY. And for a good minute I stood there, staring at the sign, debating in my head whether or not I qualified as an "authorized person" before finally walking through.

It was already unbearably hot and humid. We might as well have been swimming in the nearby Delaware River. Vermeil had invited 120 players to camp, about 85 of whom had not been on the team before. He gathered us on the field before our first practice and said he had an open mind about every guy there, veterans and rookies. From this point forward, he told us, every decision he made about our chances of making the team were based on how hard we worked, how we reacted to his coaching, his assistants' coaching, and our teammates. Vermeil is a passionate man who was—and still is—just as quick to hug a player and cry with him as he is to chew him out. But he'll do them both full tilt. He's the kind of guy you want to follow because you believe what he says; he won't lie to you for his own or the team's benefit.

That's what the Eagles' owner at the time, Leonard Tose, saw in him. Tose was watching the Rose Bowl on New Year's Day and struggling to find a new coach, someone who would be his fourth new hire in just six years of owning the team. He'd interviewed some heavyweight names such as Hank

Stram, who'd won Super Bowl IV with the Chiefs, as well as Hall of Fame quarterback Norm van Brocklin and ex-Giants coach Allie Sherman. All of them had track records as winners, but Tose wanted more than proven winners. He wanted fresh ideas and an overhaul of the team's attitude. As Vermeil's UCLA team upset top-ranked Ohio State, Tose saw a close-up of the young college coach on his screen. He'd never heard of him, but he saw a fire that practically burned an image on his television. Tose was sitting with the Eagles' GM, Jim Murray, and told Murray, "Let's talk to that guy."

Vermeil was born and raised in Calistoga, California, in Napa Valley. He went to San Jose State, spent some time coaching in the NFL with the Los Angeles Rams, and was coaching at UCLA. He wasn't all that interested in leaving a winning program in his home state for a historically losing franchise three thousand miles away. But Tose could be a persuasive man. You don't keep your millions by accepting no as an answer to a business proposition. So after three interviews—in which it seemed more like Vermeil was interviewing the Eagles than the other way around—Tose finally had his new coach.

Tose was an extravagant spender: he left $100 tips, served filet mignon in the press box, and once hired a fleet of limos to take family and friends to a game that was just a block away. He flew in a helicopter with Eagles wings painted on it and he won and lost millions as a gambler. If Vermeil had told him that giving every veteran on the roster a $1 million raise would turn the Eagles into winners, Tose would have done it.

But Vermeil chose a different path. He was a tireless worker.

Effort was in his blood. His father owned the Owl Garage in Calistoga, so named because Louie Vermeil was there night and day working on cars. Often, Vermeil was there, too, working beside his father, getting them to perform at their peak. In 1983, years after I was done playing and Vermeil had retired from the Eagles because of burnout, I spent some time trying to figure him out. I read an article in *Sports Illustrated*. It seemed, like me, Vermeil's drive came from trying to please a demanding father. His dad didn't offer many compliments when Vermeil was growing up, but he had plenty of critiques. Vermeil told *SI* that if he had thrown three touchdown passes in a high school game and came home to tell his father, Louie would tell him to go change a flat. Of course, Louie couldn't brag enough about his son to friends and neighbors, but Vermeil never knew about that. The only thing he knew his father appreciated was hard work. In that *SI* story I learned that Louie Vermeil worked for twenty-four hours straight once, just because he was fascinated with the concept of trying it. So that's what Vermeil did, too. From his very first job as a high school coach—when he worked other jobs fixing cars, digging swimming pools, and driving an ice cream truck—just to make ends meet. After he had taken the UCLA job and was finishing out the season with the Rams, he interviewed his assistants at the end of his pro workday, which was usually after midnight.

Hard work was how he decided to build the Eagles, too: One of the dozens of sayings he had posted around the locker room was "The Best Way to Kill Time Is to Work It to Death."

I didn't know what to expect that first day. The night before I lay in my bed at the Widener dorms and had no fears at all. I had been more nervous trying out for the Bell. To me, that seemed like a chance to prove to everyone who ever doubted me that I could be a great athlete. Trying out for the Eagles was just gravy. I was getting $200 a week to practice with a professional team. I was pretty pleased just being invited. Not that I slept very well. I was so excited I tossed and turned. Every time I drifted off I woke up with a start and checked the time, calculating how many more minutes there were until the 6:30 wake-up call for practice. Eventually, I just turned the clock toward the wall so I wouldn't have to face it anymore.

My roommate, Larry Marshall, set a good example for approaching camp. He was a third-year returner; we called him Fumble Larry because he actually never fumbled the ball. He was so good at reading the arc of a punt he could catch it behind his back. Fumble Larry was as calm as could be the night before camp. I was impressed that he had the kinds of books lining his shelves that would be read by educated men, not the trashy novels I had brought with me. I also appreciated the fact he didn't mock me when we first met. He just nodded his head up and down, laughed, and said, "All right, Rook."

Vermeil designed that first training camp to be as brutal as possible. He wanted to separate the guys just looking to pick up a paycheck from the guys who wanted to play. Anyone who was not dedicated would quit. He had inherited a team that had not won in a decade and had lost the will to win. The stench of losing permeated the team and the entire locker room. And Vermeil knew that before he could win, he had to reestablish that desire. The camp had to be so over the top and demanding it would separate the players. Those just there to say they were at an NFL training camp would cut themselves. And they did. Every night three or four guys streamed out of the dorms after dinner clutching their suitcases in their hands. No one on the Eagles had released them; they were releasing themselves.

Vermeil had nothing to lose doing it that way. The first day of camp he told all of us, "I don't care if you played eight or nine years in the league. If you were part of this team last year, you were terrible. The fact you are returning means nothing to me because you are returning from a lousy team. All you've proven is that you can be part of something bad. You have to show me you can be part of something good." He identified that as his mission statement from the beginning. He knew this team would not win on talent. He had to start with players who had a desire to win and then, over time, would bring in better players. Besides, how much worse could the team get if Vermeil kept the players who had always been on losing teams or found new ones, who weren't quite as good, but had a passion for playing the game? Another time, another place, another coach, and I don't get the chance that I do. But I happened to be there the summer that Dick Vermeil decided he didn't care what anyone's credentials were, he cared only about finding forty-five guys who wanted to play football the way he coached them.

Vermeil had to rebuild from top to bottom. The Eagles weren't exactly a first-class organization back then. There was still lingering dissent from the 1974 player strike. Film projectors didn't always work in the team meeting rooms. Screens would fall from the ceiling when they were pulled too hard. We all squinted watching film because there were no shades on the windows to block out the sun.

At most NFL training camps, players go in full pads for one practice a day, and for the other practice they go in shoulder pads, helmets, and shorts. During those lighter workouts players just run through plays and get their timing down. They're not full contact. But with Vermeil there was never a lighter session. He woke us up every morning by pulling the fire alarm. Then we had to walk half a mile uphill in our pads from the locker room to the practice fields. We called it the Bataan Death March. One morning a group of us were walking up the hill and we were practically comatose—it looked as if we were just aimlessly wandering. Then one of the guys yelled out, "Moo." Suddenly we all started mooing, because that's what we felt like: cows going off to the slaughter.

Vermeil even posted a sign in the locker room that read, NOBODY EVER DROWNED IN SWEAT. Every practice was almost three hours long, in the broiling sun with full pads. Guys were passing out. They were puking. They only time we were allowed water was during a break in the sessions. Vermeil had purposely invited so many players to camp so he'd have long lines during drills, because those were the only times players were going to get a break. He wouldn't let up, which meant I couldn't let up. I gave every ounce. I didn't know if that would be enough to make the team, but I wanted to make it real hard for the coaches to cut me. I caught every ball that came my way. Then I would take the ball and sprint thirty or forty yards downfield, causing all the fans to scream.

Denny and I encouraged each other to go full speed all the time. Practice how you play, that was our motto. Every time I sprinted downfield after a practice catch it made Vermeil turn around and pay attention to me, but it pissed the other players in camp off to no end. Most of the veteran receivers would catch a ball in practice and jog back to the huddle. But most of them weren't trying to prove themselves the way I was. The practices had a lot of the veterans complaining in the locker room, and what the veterans did the rookies did. But I just kept my mouth shut. I may have been a rookie, but I was thirty years old and had been a member of the union. I trusted nobody. So when somebody started moaning I looked the other way. I was just there to try out. I didn't need to become anyone's best friend or whining partner until I made the team. Denny and I both talked about how the physical aspects of camp were nothing compared to the stress of waiting it out and wondering if the next day would be our last day.

In the mornings we started with pass-catching drills such as the machine gun, where coaches threw balls at you one after the other. As soon as you caught one, the next one was in the air. Or they threw it underhand as fast as they could, like they were pitching in fast-pitch softball, which made the oblong ball spin awkwardly. My favorite was the toe tap, when we'd make over-the-shoulder catches on the sideline and try to keep both feet in bounds. When we did that I was just Tommy McDonald in my backyard, doing what I had done a thousand times before. Denny had a theory, which he had learned from his father, that we both applied to practices: Fight the biggest guy at camp just once, and your reputation as a tough guy will be set. I didn't take it literally, I just tried to get my reps against the best defensive backs on the team whenever I could. Denny, however, did what his daddy said. When a reporter asked Denny what he wanted to do most, Denny answered, "Knock Bill Bergey on his ass." Bergey was our Pro Bowl middle linebacker and as nasty as practices were long. Guys who were long shots to make the team didn't call out Bill Bergey in the newspapers. But Denny figured going after Bergey would impress the coaches. So during one play early in training camp he popped Bill as hard as he could. Bergey told him, Ease up, it's just a practice. Denny did, and then Bill came up through the middle and knocked Denny flat on his ass. Denny was so mad that on the next play Bergey could see Denny's knuckles turning white because he was ready to launch out of his stance and hit him. When the play started, Denny jumped and Bill sidestepped like a matador. But at least the coaches were keeping an eye on Denny.

Even if they missed something during practice, the coaches would catch everything later that night. They filmed every practice, and every move we made in practice. They'd shoot our feet, our hips, our hands, our butts, our shoulders, and then our whole bodies. At night after dinner, we'd be dead tired. But Vermeil made us watch the film from that day to see how we could improve the most minor details of our games.

While Vermeil almost never encouraged us at first—when it came to him we subscribed to the adage "If he's not criticizing he doesn't care"—the receivers' coach, Dick Coury, kept us somewhat sane. He had been the head coach of the Portland Storm in the WFL and was a brilliant offensive coach. He had seven kids and infinite patience. He had a warm smile and a calming influence on all of us when it seemed nothing else was going right. I was so low on the depth chart that my name was written in masking tape on top of my locker, and it was spelled incorrectly, with an *i* at the end of it instead of an *e*. In the heat of camp you're just looking for a bone to hold on to, just one positive thing to get you through the night that you can take into the next day. After that first week, even if everything about my footwork, route running, and hand placement were wrong, Coury would tell me he thought I was practicing like an All-Pro.

He didn't know it at the time, but Coury also provided me with more than just comforting words. He supplied a mole in the coaches' offices. One of Coury's kids, a teenage son named Tim, was hanging out at camp and I befriended him. He reminded me of my students and it was easy for me to lapse into that teacher-student patter that I had become so good at over the years. I saw him admiring my car one day—a stick-shift Datsun 260Z—and I offered to teach him how to drive it.

Once he became pretty good at it and I didn't have to worry about his ruining my clutch, I let him drive it around. There was a beer garden and deli called The Campus Casino on the Widener campus and Tim would get a bunch of us hoagies that we'd scarf down after meetings. Tim also hung out with his dad and Vermeil in a lot of the coaches meetings. In exchange for using my car, he told me where I stood on the depth chart and what coaches were saying about me. I knew when they loved a hustle play I had made or were frustrated my route running wasn't getting better. I never really sweated those first couple of cuts because Tim had told me what the coaches thought of me.

Reporters noticed my practice habits, too. They came up to me and told me they could tell that I wanted it worse than anyone on the field. They said I played like a guy who had just come down from the 700-level at the Vet, which is exactly what I was. We were such a bad team, with so few good stories, that a lot of reporters focused on me that training camp. I was like a circus freak and when interviewed I'd jokingly bark out, "Step right this way, folks. Come and see the tattooed lady and the thirty-year-old rookie." Because Widener is so close to Glenolden, every practice there would be thirty people from the neighborhood cheering me on. My dad was always there, along with several aunts, uncles, and cousins. They were going nuts, every time I caught a pass or just finished a drill. One of them would go home and say, "Hey, I saw Vince at practice today and he looks good." The next day there'd more people who wanted to see it themselves.

But the attention didn't exactly endear me to my team-mates at first. They derisively called me Sandlot. The veteran players especially did not take me seriously—I was someone who could potentially take the job of one of their friends—and just seemed to resent me. The team was never going to build around me, they rightfully thought. So who was this guy? How did he get here? Is he just some publicity stunt for the team? They definitely felt the amount of attention I was getting was disproportionate to my experience and skill. One afternoon Ray Didinger, the Hall of Fame sportswriter for the *Philadelphia Bulletin,* was standing in the team cafeteria wait-ing to interview someone. One of the players walked by him and snidely said, "Doing another Papale story today, Ray?"

I took a lot of cheap shots during practice. It seemed like I was always double-teamed, always getting knocked down, always getting up and then getting knocked down again. And they all hurt in some way. But nothing that I needed treatment for, or at least nothing I said I needed treatment for. Rookies trying to make the team never go to the training room unless they are get-ting taped. That's rule number one in professional football. You don't pull muscles; you don't pull up lame. The first week I saw a couple rookies in the training room and heard coaches making comments and after that I would have needed my leg amputated before I spent a minute missing practice because of an injury.

But I did become pretty paranoid about getting taken out. And suddenly I was playing passively. Especially after one play, when another rookie came up to me and said, "You snitched on me, so every time you come off the line, I'm gonna clobber you. Every shot I get, I'll take." I had no idea what he was talking about. I was too afraid of the coaches to actually talk to them. If some guy in rough touch or semi-pro had said that to me, I would have thrown a ball at the guy and gone after him. But I didn't want to leave the impression that I was some loose cannon who couldn't handle a challenge. Suddenly how to handle the guys who were coming after me caused me more anxiety than what these guys might do to me. I asked Marshall for some help and, typically, he shrugged it off, telling me that I had had it pretty good so far and "as a rookie didn't have anything to complain about." Finally I told Dick Coury what I was thinking and he put me at ease. "Vince," he said. "The question of guts has never come up in our discussions about you."

One afternoon, during our third week of practice, I took a hit that I did worry would knock me out of camp. I ran a curl route, one-on-one against a cornerback named Clifford Brooks. After I caught the pass I relaxed for just a second before making my break and taking my forty-yard sprint downfield. As much as the veteran receivers hated that habit because it made them look lazy, the defensive backs hated it because they felt it showed them up. As I slowed down, Brooks came up from behind me and threw me down to the grass. All my body weight came down on the point of my right shoulder. I felt a sharp pain immediately, but I was so ticked I shot right back up and popped Brooks in the face mask. We were separated before it escalated, but I had to defend myself. As a rookie you can't turn around to a coach and say, "Did you see what he did?" Then you get a rep as a complainer. Rookies have no rights on the field. We were even in a separate section of the locker room that was caged off. And I had no football résumé. The World League was a joke to these guys.

As I walked back to the huddle my shoulder was throbbing. I rotated it around like a windmill a few times and continued on with practice. I wouldn't find out until later in the season that I had a first-degree shoulder separation.

Later that week we had our first scrimmage against another NFL team, the New York Jets, at their Hofstra training camp on Long Island. At this point a lot of guys, not just on the Eagles but within the press, kept thinking that the coaches would eventually come to their senses and realize they could not keep a thirty-year-old rookie. But this was the turning point for me. Not to make the team, but to at least gain some legitimacy in the eyes of my teammates. It wasn't a full-blown game, just a controlled scrimmage with minimal hitting. But it was against a regular secondary of players I didn't know who were looking to impress their coaches as much as I was. Unlike our practices, this defense had no idea what was coming; and I didn't know what they had planned for us.

I needed just two plays to make an impression. On the first, the play call was for me to run a quick post, which entails running seven yards upfield making a strong plant with my outside foot, then digging diagonally toward the goal posts. By the time I make my cut, the ball should be in the air. I swore I would drive to the post like no receiver in history. It would be one, two, three steps, plant the foot, push off hard, and be gone. Coming out of the huddle I visualized, just as I did at St. Joe's and just as I did before running that forty to make the Bell. I saw the safety coming up to hit me after I made the catch and then I saw myself lowering my shoulder and blasting right through him. I caught the ball, then I did just that. And ran forty yards to the end zone without ever turning around. The coaches and the players loved that.

Later that practice we were doing an eleven-on-eleven drill. Full offense verses full defense. I ran a fly pattern, just a straight sprint along the sideline for the corner of the end zone. As I was running I recognized the quarterback had thrown the ball over my opposite shoulder. I had to adjust mid-sprint and made the catch with my back to the quarterback, à la Willie Mays' basket catch in the 1954 World Series. As I walked off the field I saw a guy walking toward me. He had pearly white teeth, long black hair, and looked like someone I had seen a thousand times but couldn't remember where. He stopped me when we passed to say, "Hey, number eighty-three, great catch. That was a major-league catch." Then I realized Joe Namath had just given me a compliment. I was so proud, if I had been cut right there it wouldn't have mattered.

Things just kept getting better. I was feeling so comfortable that, when Vermeil allowed everyone to bring their families down for a big team dinner one night, I invited Sandy to join us. We had spoken pretty frequently on the phone and she had been encouraging when I needed it.

By the middle of August I was feeling pretty good about my chances, even without any inside information from Tim

Coury. I just looked around and saw there were fewer and fewer receivers in camp, yet I was still there. Then, before a game in Miami, Vermeil gave me a chance to seal the deal. The morning of the game Vermeil came up to me and said, "Harold's not feeling right and you'll be starting. Are you ready? Do you know the playbook?" I said I did. Then he told me I'd be playing the whole first half.

Suddenly I was incredibly nervous. I tried to tell myself to calm down, that I had nothing to lose. But, for the first time in camp, I knew that I did. This game was going back live to Philly. Everyone I knew would be watching. But, more important, a dream was within reach. I could make this team. No, I *would* make this team. Unless I screwed up. My shoulder was still hurting, but I told myself I could do anything for thirty minutes on a football field. I sensed this was a turning point in my life, not just because of a chance to make the Eagles, but for the opportunities it would bring. I thought of all that in the moments that Vermeil walked away.

We were playing a night game, and those were the worst. On game day you just wanted to wake up, eat breakfast, and get to the stadium. Having an eight o'clock game made the whole day interminable. We were staying at the Doral Hotel, so I went down to the pool with my playbook to relax. I was conscious of everything I did knowing that this could be the last time I had an experience like this. I tried to soak up as much atmosphere as I could. Fortunately, there happened to be a lingerie show going on by the pool, so that helped me relax.

Another thing happened when I got to the game that made me feel at home. As I jogged onto the Orange Bowl field I heard someone in the stands yelling, "Vincie, Vincie!" This was more than just a fan. Only people from Glenolden called me Vincie. When I got closer I realized it was Mike Paynter, who had knocked me unconscious when we were playing Pee Wee football in fifth grade. Seeing him just helped me relax, it reminded me where I had come from and how far I had gotten, and whether I made the team or not, I had done something remarkable.

Vermeil had told me that he would be throwing to me early in the game, and he did. I was really into the rhythm of the game. At one point during a huddle, the other receiver announced he didn't know what to do on the play that had just been called. It was a run to his side and I told him to switch sides with me and be a decoy. I filled his role as the backside blocker on a sweep and hit Dolphins safety Tim Foley so hard he flipped head over feet. That whole game I felt like I was being rewarded for my effort from day to day and week to week. I wasn't perfect. During the game our tight end Richie Osborne told me I was tipping off plays by keeping my head down when I was a blocker and picking it up when I was going into a pattern. But after the game, quarterback Mike Boryla said he could sense the confidence I had in myself and he felt himself becoming more confident in me. When a reporter from the Philly *Daily News* asked him about my age, Boryla shrugged him off: "So he's thirty. I hope Vince turns out to be the oldest rookie in the league."

We got back to Philly and went over the game film the next day. Vermeil turned on the projector and, on the screen, in front of the entire team, were highlights of plays I had made the night before. There was an entire section of the film devoted to my efforts. My first catch, my block on Foley, my sprinting down the field to make plays on special teams. He said that this was the type of personality and attitude he wanted this team to have. "This guy is a rookie," Vermeil continued. "He has no right being here. He was just in training camp to make the lines long. But he is going to make this football team."

Now guys like Harold Carmichael started giving me pointers during practice on how to run my routes. Bill Bradley, a veteran safety, told me how not to tip off the plays I was running. Bill Bergey and fellow linebacker John Bunting teased me that the only way I could practice and play with the intensity I did was if I were on speed. When Coury or Vermeil made points to me while watching film they were about improving, not just criticisms. They wanted to make me a better football player because that would make the Eagles a better football team. My entire persona had changed. I was bursting with confidence. I approached every practice as if I belonged. If it was possible, I had more enthusiasm than I had had before.

In September, the last game of the preseason, we played the Patriots and I kept getting on the field. At that point in training camp our top two wideouts, Carmichael and Charlie Smith, were still banged up. So I was shuttling between playing on the scout team and taking snaps with our first team. I could barely move at the end of practice but at least the coaches were getting plenty of chances to see me.

Early in the second half against the Pats I was told to run an out pattern. But when I lined up I recognized the Pats were in a zone. The cornerback had the short route and the safety had the deep route. If I ran the out as called, the corner would jump on the pass because he didn't have to worry about protecting deep. At the line of scrimmage the quarterback and I made sight adjustments, meaning we both recognized the zone and decided I would run a fade up the sideline. Our quarterback, Johnny Walton, would have to throw a touch pass in the empty space between the cornerback and safety. Johnny led me too much and I caught the ball, but was way out of bounds. Out of nowhere came New England safety Tim Fox, who was also a rookie. Unlike me, however, he had been an All-American at Ohio State and a first-round draft pick. He put his elbow under my chinstrap and my head snapped back. I bit my tongue, had some teeth knocked loose, and felt blood dripping out of my mouth. But the rules rookies follow about avoiding the training room also apply to blood. It's not going to keep you out of the game. Instead, as I walked off the field, I wiped some of the blood from my mouth onto my pants. There is nothing better than having blood on your pants when you are playing football. It builds your persona. I just imagined I was Tommy McDonald, that's what he would have done.

From the sidelines I bided my time, waiting for payback.

Late in the game, I got it. We were running a sweep to my side of the field. I was the crackback guy, taking out any defensive backs who tried to get in the way. Sure enough, here comes Fox. He never even saw me. I just ripped him from his blindside. It was cold-blooded, but that was the game.

Now Denny and I stayed up late talking about the little things that might make us better. He had short arms, so we figured out how some of the martial arts stuff we learned in the spring might help him keep defensive ends from locking on his pads. And we talked a lot about ear holing people on special teams. That was when we were running downfield and gave the opponent a headslap right on his ear that would make his head spin. Special teams was the perfect place for both of us, because we loved hitting as much as anything else in football.

The regular season began on September 12 in Dallas. The Monday before that game was called Blue Monday throughout the NFL. That was the last cut-down day. I arrived for practice early that morning and I took a long, slow walk through the locker room. My stall was in the far corner of the room, the farthest away from the entrance, and I looked around at all the names above the lockers. It had been four months since that first tryout in April, when I was so overwhelmed with being in there that I nearly missed the tryout entirely. Now I had spent the summer practicing with the guys I used to cheer for. And I felt as though I could play at their level.

As I approached my locker I was looking for a sign that

I had made the team. I saw one right away. There was a plastic nameplate above my stall—no more masking tape—and my name was spelled correctly.

But I still hadn't heard from Vermeil. I put my practice gear on and walked out onto the field. It was a gorgeous September day. We were doing our pre-practice stretches and I had visions of these All-Pro Cowboys running in my head. I saw Roger Staubach and Ed "Too Tall" Jones and Harvey Martin. Then I saw Vermeil walking through the tunnel, and all those Cowboys disappeared. He always had a hop in his gait, as if he couldn't wait to get where he was going, and a big smile on his face. Every practice, you felt like there was no place in the world he would rather be. As Vermeil got closer to the group I was loosening up with, I ran through a mental checklist: Nameplate on the locker? Check. One less receiver than the day before? Check. Word from the coach I had made the team? Not yet.

Even as he put his hand out to shake mine I was sure he was going to cut me. My heart was beating too fast for someone who was standing still. He had made a mistake. I'd had a nice run. But it was over. That's what I was thinking he'd tell me when we finally shook hands. I stood up to walk into the tunnel, to retrieve and give back my playbook. I don't remember sticking my hand out to shake his, but I must have been leaning forward because he had to stop me from walking past him. Then he said, "Congratulations, old man, you are a Philadelphia Eagle."

I went batty right there on the field. I told Vermeil he better not be screwing with me. He laughed and said he wasn't, that

I had earned it. Practice was about to start, but I had one thing I had to do. I asked Vermeil if I could go make a phone call.

"Who are you going to call?" he asked. "The AP?"

"No," I said. "My dad."

There was a pay phone just inside the tunnel that led to the locker room. Standing in my cleats and shoulder pads I dialed up the plant at Westinghouse. Slim Kaufman was a shop steward right out of central casting—tall and slim. When he answered the phone I said, "Tell Kingie that his little boy is an Eagle."

I held the phone to my ear and listened as Slim yelled the news. The whole factory erupted in cheers.

NINE

EOPLE GAVE me a hard time for chasing a boy's dream when I was thirty years old. But my argument to them was always the same: I'm not married, don't have kids, and have a job I can go back to. Nothing was holding me back— why shouldn't I have taken one last shot to pursue something I loved? But I had no idea how much my life would change once I made it.

I had a contract for $21,000, plus a signing bonus of $3,000. Big money as far as I was concerned, big enough that I could get my own furnished apartment for $450 a month on a golf course. I even had a deck overlooking a swimming pool. For the first time in my life I was living alone and had money in my pocket to burn.

After making the team, Harold Carmichael took me to Boyds, an upscale men's store, to go shopping for a new suit.

Carmichael was six-eight, a silky smooth receiver who knew what it was like to be the underdog, believe it or not. He'd been just a seventh-round pick of the Eagles in 1971. That first year he blew out his knee and the second year the coaches didn't know what to do with him. They just didn't have the imagination to consider putting someone that tall at wide receiver and instead lined him up at tight end. Finally, in 1973, one of the coaches had the bright idea to put him on the outside, where no one was tall enough to guard him. The result: Carmichael led the league with 67 receptions and 1,116 yards. He'd catch at least one pass in every game he played for the next seven seasons.

Being one of the few reasons to watch the Eagles, Carmichael was treated like a hero when he walked into Boyds that afternoon. But no one really noticed me. It wasn't surprising, since I was unshaven, had on a T-shirt, and had been celebrating the fact I'd made the team for what seemed like forty-eight hours straight. For about half an hour I browsed through the racks, checking out some cool duds, wondering how I would spend the $3,000 in cash I had burning a hole in my pocket. Eventually Carmichael strolled over to me and said, "Anyone help you yet?" I told him no, at which point he looked back at the sales guys and said, "Fellas, this is my paisan Vinnie Papale. He just made the team. Isn't anyone going to help him?" All of a sudden I was treated like I was the most popular man in the store. They told me how much they loved me, how proud they were of me, and how they were rooting for me the entire time. That was nice of them, but by then it was too late. I wasn't spending my signing bonus at Boyds. It was the first time I saw how fickle and phony fame can be.

That first week of practice was performed at a different pace and different intensity than training camp. Every one of those days at Widener was about proving yourself, beating out your teammates, getting your coach's attention, and getting better. The coaches didn't think about opponents. But once we were into the regular season, there was very little time for individual improvement. At that point we were who we were. All we could do was practice the game plan the coaches came up with and try not to screw up on Sundays.

While I led the team in receiving during the preseason, I knew what my role was: special teams and scout team. I wouldn't see much action on the field as a receiver. Leading up to the Cowboys game I emulated the moves of their All-Pro receiver Drew Pearson. And I ran like a man on fire during our kickoff and punt coverage practices. Most teams practice their special teams coverage during the last fifteen minutes of practice. We were no different. But while on other squads that session might be when the intensity winds down, that was when it picked up for us. Until the 1970s, special teams had been seen as nothing more than a transition from offense to defense, or a chance for the kickers to screw up a field goal. But Vermeil had been the league's first special-teams coach, when he worked for Hall of Famer George Allen on the Rams in 1969. Vermeil, with his infectious, high-energy style, was perfect for the job. Special teamers are on the field for about only fifteen plays at the most per game. While the majority of football collisions happen in a confined space near the line of scrimmage, every special teams hit comes at the end of a full-field sprint. We are the kamikazes of professional football, hurling ourselves headfirst into walls of blockers and ball carriers coming our way. The intensity level is so high because it is the closest thing to Roman gladiator battles in football. Even the names of the positions on special teams invoke violence. The guys lined up on the outside—usually the fastest players on the team—are called gunners. The guys running down the middle are wedgebusters, their sole job being to throw their bodies into the wedge of blockers that forms in front of the return man. More than skill, special-teams play is all about effort, energy, and perseverance. I had the ideal temperament for special teams because I would not stay blocked. Often I'd overrun the return man and have to make a U-turn to come back and tackle him.

Special-teams plays are where the hardest hits and the most injuries in professional football occur. Which is why it's usually the subs playing on kick coverages. We are the most replaceable to the coaches and the most desperate to stay. If this is what is asked, this is what we'll do. On the Eagles—and on most teams—we saw it as our duty to protect our turf, literally, because if we didn't cover kickoffs and punts well, our opponents would have great field position. And during Vermeil's first couple of seasons, we couldn't afford to give other teams any more advantages than they already had. Plus, the combo of Vermeil's being the league's first special-teams coach and his being a product of George Allen's system made him more manic about this aspect of the game than most. Allen believed you hadn't studied film until you knew it backward as well as you knew it forward, and Vermeil agreed. He had us watching film incessantly. And he was often in there with us, preaching about the importance of field position with every new reel we watched. He'd have us examine how players positioned themselves if they were going to rush the punter; how every player lined up in kickoffs to give us a clue as to how they were setting up their blocks, whether they were to the right, left, or down the middle. Were they going to attack or drop back with the runner? The most minute tics of a team made the difference to him, and therefore to us. Kenny Iman, our special-teams coach, used to take it one step further. If learning every movement of our opponent hadn't prepared us, Iman would tack up pictures of the other team's most dangerous special teams guys so we could see their faces every day.

Everything Vermeil did was about effort and professionalism, even the last fifteen minutes of practice. Vermeil's practices didn't let up during the season. They were still almost three hours long. If any of us slowed down, that was it, we were done. Someone else was on the street ready to take our jobs. Vermeil coined the phrase "Eagle Effort" and never stopped invoking words like character and sacrifice. There wasn't a player on the team who didn't believe Vermeil was talking directly to him every time he gave a speech.

EXPECTATIONS WEREN'T HIGH for us when we traveled to Dallas that opening weekend of the 1976 season. The Eagles had just come off a 4–10 season, had a new coach, and hadn't acquired any players who made other teams in the league tremble. In fact, I was the highest profile addition to the Eagles roster, and to a lot of people that only proved how desperate the struggling team really was.

The Cowboys, meanwhile, were in the midst of their reign as America's Team. Everything about them was brave and valiant and big. Their quarterback was Roger Staubach, a Navy grad, a Heisman Trophy winner, everybody's All-American. In 1975 they had won the NFC title before narrowly losing the Super Bowl to the Steelers. They were clearly the class of the NFC. We were not.

Denny Franks was my roommate on the road. He had a wealthy uncle who'd made money as a Fort Worth oilman. So the Saturday night before our game, he took Denny and me and our fathers—who made the trip with us—to Baby Doe's, an old-fashioned steak place in Dallas. We were thrilled to be taken out, because it meant we could pocket the $19 in per diem the Eagles had given us. As we walked into the restaurant I saw Vermeil eating with his family. I waved and planned on walking right by, but Vermeil wouldn't have that. He called me over, introduced me to his family, and told them nice things about me. I was surprised. My image of a pro football head coach, even after two months of training camp with Vermeil, was that of a stoic leader, someone who didn't want to socialize with his players. It felt good to be acknowledged in front of Vermeil's family, and it was just one of the many reasons that I and so many of his players wanted to do well for him.

That night as Denny and I tried to fall asleep we had a long talk about how far we had come. We both wanted to be a part of turning the Eagles around very badly. Then I kept him up all night telling him stories about Bednarik and Tommy McDonald and about growing up being in love with this team, when they were winning titles and when they were losing nearly every game in a season. Denny was from Pittsburgh. Like my father, his father was a factory worker, punching a clock in a steel mill for most of his adult life. Denny understood where my passion came from, and why it meant so much to me to make it. He marveled at the fact I was going to play for my hometown team. At that point, as a backup to three positions on the offensive line, he was firmly entrenched on the team, while we both knew I was one bad game away from getting cut. As he fell asleep that night, he prayed more for me to have a good game than he did for himself.

Neither Denny nor I smoked, but we took some big drags on cigarettes before that first game. We were just looking for an edge to get us hyped up to go out there and kill ourselves. It became a tradition for us to inhale as buzz-worthy a drag as we could before every game. Then we would just sit there, staring at each other in full uniform. Our legs would be shaking, bouncing up and down like a couple of kids who had to pee. Denny would get so pumped up he'd need to release some energy before the game. He'd walk into the weight room and go a few rounds with a heavy bag.

In the end, I didn't need the cigarette to make my head spin before that first game. I was totally awed from the second

I walked onto the field. It was about 120 degrees on the turf. You could see the heat shimmering off it. When I looked around I could see the Dallas Cowboy cheerleaders, Staubach, the great defensive linemen Harvey Martin and Ed "Too Tall" Jones. Then there was Tom Landry, whose profile looked as though it belonged on the side of a mountain. He had the demeanor to match. I was so nervous it was tough to breathe; I actually didn't during that opening kickoff. I was acutely aware of every sensation as I ran down the field—the noise of the crowd, the grunts, the groans, the speed, the collisions—and it all almost made me stop dead in my tracks.

Later that day Denny and I compared when the ball is kicked to the moment when a stick of dynamite is lit. The length of time it takes to run down the field is how long the wick burns, and then that first hit is the huge explosion. The intensity had picked up to an extreme that I had never felt before. It was nothing I could identify with from life or sports. Not my mom's illness, not feeling poor, not drifting through the air after a pole vault, and not two months of training camp and preseason games. The full spectrum of colors did not have a shade for how intense that first play felt. I didn't think it could be more intense than that, until I jogged off the field and was met face-to-face by Vermeil.

I was supposed to shed the two blockers covering me on the outside and tackle the ball carrier. But I didn't let my intuition guide me. I got too caught up in the emotion and wrestled with the blockers instead. Vermeil came over to have what I called a come-to-Jesus meeting. He yelled at me for such lackadaisical coverage, which I could take. Then he said to me, "I didn't stick my neck out for you for that kind of coverage."

When it came time to make cuts during training camp the coaches would sit around a long table and throw out their suggestions. Inevitably my name would come up and it was usually Vermeil who said, "No, he's a character guy, we need character guys on this team." He had fought the hardest for me, and not because he needed the publicity, but because he expected me to provide this team with an example of how lucky we all were to be playing, that it was something that shouldn't be taken for granted. If I lost Vermeil, I lost my job. Right there on the sideline I fast-forwarded to getting cut, all because I couldn't get my head of out my ass long enough to stop being psyched out and just cover a kickoff. Now that I'd made the team, that wasn't how I saw my career ending.

After Vermeil's pep talk Denny sat down next to me on the bench. He reminded me to settle down, let myself take some hits so I could recognize that I was in the damn game, and then go finish the job. He told me not to let my dream die that day. We punted a lot that day, and the rest of the game I didn't let a coverage go by where I wasn't the first guy down the field. I may not have made the tackle, but I was always around the ball. We lost the game, 27–7, but at least I wouldn't lose my job.

WHEN VERMEIL WAS George Allen's Rams special-teams coach, Allen gave his group of kamikazes color televisions if they made especially big hits. Other teams didn't bother with gifts; they just paid bounties. Tackles inside the fifteen-yard line were awarded with a $50 bonus, a recovered fumble was worth $100. But by the time Vermeil took over the Eagles, blatantly paying players bounties was no longer allowed. Instead, players started pools, which is something players still do today. Deion Sanders once talked about how, when he was playing, they'd put $100 in a hat and if someone knocked someone else out, they got the money. In our pool, all the receivers put in $5 if one of us had a touchdown catch. A knock-down block was worth a couple of bucks. A big hit by a receiver on special teams was worth the same as a touchdown. And if Larry Marshall returned a punt or kickoff all the way, that was big money. At the end of the season we had a pile of about $3,000, which we split among the five receivers and then spent at a place called the Latin Casino in Cherry Hill. We had a massive dinner at Bookbinders and then went to see Donna Summer in concert.

But our special-teams coaches, Ken Iman and Rod Rust, also came up with a way to give us an incentive: the "Who's Nuts?" Award. This was supposed to give us an identity that was separate from the team. As if we needed more motivation than just staying employed. And the week before the Dallas game they unveiled their plan. Iman had T-shirts made with the words "WHO'S NUTS?" printed across the top, above the flying Eagles logo. Every week, in the locker room as soon as the game ended, the coaches would bestow the special-teams player who had made the biggest impact in the game with the award, which included the T-shirt, of course, but also the admiration of teammates. Win or lose, someone on special teams would be told they did all they could that day. To us, these were more important than getting game balls, which sometimes went to everyone from the team MVP that day to a friend of the owner's. But only one guy got the WHO'S NUTS? T-shirt.

The competition was intense, especially between Denny and me. On punt teams, he was the snapper, which meant getting steamrolled by two defensive linemen every time he hiked the ball. On kickoffs he was a wedgebuster. His job was to line up next to the kicker, sprint down the middle of the field, and take out at least two of the other team's lead blockers at the same time. One wasn't enough. Even taking out just two implied his effort wasn't there. He loved it as much as I did. We were just a couple of sons of factory workers. We were such kindred spirits our fathers had become great friends. They would tailgate before the game, sit together during the game, and then go out drinking with us after the game. Usually one of them would buy the bar a round, because they were so proud of their boys.

That first weekend, after the Dallas game, Iman and Rust gave me the Who's Nuts? Award. I was surprised, considering I thought Vermeil was going to cut me after the opening kickoff. But when they reviewed the games on film they saw I recovered from my jitters and played with the same fearlessness I had shown during training camp. I was so proud of the T-shirt that I wore it under my pads on game day for the rest of the season.

Our next game was our home opener, against the Giants. For as long as both the Eagles and Giants had been in the NFL, they had been each other's biggest rivals. One of the most famous hits in the history of pro football was in 1960, when Chuck Bednarik laid out Giants running back Frank Gifford. It was in November at Yankee Stadium, and the two players personified the teams they represented. Bednarik was Concrete Charley, the last of the sixty-minute men who played both offense and defense. One exhibition game he tore his biceps muscle and, instead of sitting out a meaningless game, told the team doctor to tape it up so he could get back on the field. Gifford was a handsome, famous, fleet-footed running back who had starred at USC. As soon as the Giants made him their number-one pick in the 1952 NFL draft, he became the face of the franchise, leading them to the NFL title in 1956.

When the two teams met that November afternoon in 1960, first place was on the line. The Eagles were 6–1; the Giants 5–1–1. Late in the game the Eagles were up 17–10, but the Giants were threatening. Gifford caught a pass and then—*wham*—Bednarik hit him going full speed in the opposite direction. Eagles players remembered the sound as being unlike anything they had ever heard on the field. It wasn't the normal thud of pads on pads. It was a crack. The way Gifford fell to the ground they thought he was dead.

He was, in fact, unconscious, and the ball rolled out of his arms and was recovered by Eagles linebacker Chuck Weber, clinching the game for the Eagles. The image that will last forever, though, is of Bednarik, standing over the motionless Gifford, pumping his fist in celebration. Gifford suffered such a severe concussion that he missed the rest of the 1960 season and all of 1961.

In 1976, both teams were far removed from their glory years. The Giants were one of the few teams the Eagles were good enough to beat in 1975. But the hatred for each other was still there. As much, if not more, for me. Just one game into my pro career I still had to remind myself to stay focused on the fact that I was playing against the Giants, not rooting against them.

This was the first time I was playing in front of my paisanos. It was also Dick Vermeil's first home game and I was pumped. The starting lineups were announced and the PA announcer said, "And now introducing the rest of your Philadelphia Eagles." Most of the guys jogged out of the tunnel toward our sideline, where they stopped. But I sprinted like I was running the 100 meters in the Olympics and didn't stop until I got to the other end of the field. I had my arms raised in the air, and as I neared the end zone at that side of the stadium I pointed my fingers toward the 700-level, exactly where I had sat the season before, and where Chuck Gardner and Billy Thomas were sitting on that day. The crowd went nuts. And for this game there weren't any nerves at all. We won the toss and had the ball first. But at the end of that drive we had to punt. Our punter, Spike Jones, kicked a beauty that went fifty yards. I beat a double-team block, hustled downfield, and nailed the ball carrier. The Giants' biggest threat for that game was Larry Csonka, back in the NFL after his half season making more than a million dollars in the WFL. But our defense was all over him. He'd gain just thirty-three yards on ten carries. Meanwhile, our offense was having its way with the Giants, opening up a 10–0 lead at halftime. I was having a blast, making tackles on kickoffs and racing everyone downfield on punt coverage. Late in the third quarter I beat my blocker and downed a punt on the Giants sixteen-yard line. One Giant vet kept yapping in my ear the whole time, telling me I was too old to be trying to prove I could play, asking me what I had done to get any attention. I was about to show him.

Midway through the fourth quarter we had a 13–0 lead and were driving. We had a third down on the Giants' thirty-eight-yard line, but Boryla was sacked for a loss of twelve, forcing us to punt from the fifty. There was still plenty of time left in the game to overcome less than a two-touchdown deficit, and with a good return the Giants would have excellent field position and a chance to cut the lead in half. Spike Jones had a leg with as much control as a sand wedge. If he said he was going to land the ball in a particular spot with a certain amount of backspin, that's pretty much what he did. He told me to get to the numbers on the ten-yard line. It's a cardinal sin for a punt returner to field the ball from within the ten, so if I could get there chances were good I'd have a free shot at downing the ball, giving the Giants horrible field position.

I was the gunner and as soon as I stepped off the line after the snap I was double-teamed. The two Giants tried to force me outside but I kept my lean and just drove as hard as I could. I was running and leaning, running and leaning, as if the sideline were the edge of a cliff I was trying to avoid. They were swinging their forearms in my face and I was grabbing them by the shirts and trying to yank them down while catapulting myself past them. The three of us battled like this for more than forty yards downfield, never letting go of one another.

I had actually lost track of the ball and, for the first time as a pro, I experienced the sensation of playing the game in a vacuum. Most guys say they never hear the crowd during a play. But that hadn't been the case for me, especially in Dallas, where I heard every sound acutely. But on this play, all I heard was my heart beating and the wind coming through my ear holes. I kept leaning, driving the blockers backward, and I could feel them starting to give. I looked down at my feet and saw we were around the fifteen-yard line and I dug harder, trying to get as low as possible so I could sneak through the small space between their shins and get to the ball.

My head was down and then it felt like we had all hit a wall. I look up and see one of the players who had been blocking me tumbling down, right into Jimmy Robinson, the Giants' punt returner. The collision occurred just as Robinson tried catching the ball, which was now skittishly bouncing around the field. I grabbed it and ran into the end zone. I was so dumbfounded by my good luck I didn't know what to do. I just handed the ball to the ref and put my palms in the air, as if asking, "Can you believe it?"

The touchdown didn't count, however, because I had been ruled down at the Giants' six-yard line. But two plays later, we scored again, putting us ahead 20–0, in a game we would win 20–7.

After the game was over, I saw my guys in the stands as I walked toward the tunnel and it was exhilarating. Fans were yelling my name. One kid chased me down and asked me for my autograph, yelling, "Mr. Papale, Mr. Papale." I got a great picture with my dad and even with some of my former students who were at the game. As I walked through the tunnel, fans asked me to throw them my wristbands and my chinstrap. In his postgame speech Vermeil never once mentioned himself. He told us how we had earned a win, and deserved the win, and that this win was for the fans of Philly, the most loyal fans in the world.

We had been winless in the preseason and this was my first time in a winning NFL locker room. And two things happened to make me feel like I had been validated as a player. I won another WHO'S NUTS? T-shirt, which I gave to George Corner, and I was invited to my first team party.

The next day Vermeil gave a speech at the Maxwell Club, an old-time Philadelphia institution among the well-heeled of the city. He was giddy about his first NFL win, so giddy, in fact, he admitted to overreacting and getting so excited he feared he wouldn't be able to prepare us for the next weekend's game. He talked about how his team won because of effort and character. "Maybe I overuse the word *character*," he said. "But I believe you win with character players. I question the loyalty of a player [Larry Csonka] who sells his services for one point five million. He'll make his money, play three years, and bail out. I'd rather have Vince Papale. He'll give you everything he's got whether he's making eighteen thousand or eighty thousand."

He was almost right. I didn't even need the $18,000.

NOW I WAS the toast of the town. A local boy made good playing for the team every kid from Philadelphia dreamed of playing for. I went from the back of every nightclub line to the front. Before I couldn't afford anything that cost full price. Now that I could, I was getting everything for free. I used to go for jogs near the stadium on South Broad Street and fans would call out my name and say, "Hey Vince, what's happening, way to go." Midway through the season I still hadn't caught a regular season pass—and wouldn't for the entire year—but fans still chanted, "Put in Papale." Philly is a big city that feels like a little town and everywhere I went people were patting me on the back, literally, acting as if I were one of the guys from their neighborhood. Essentially, I was.

Everybody wanted to hear my story: How, why, what now? Ray Didinger, the Eagles beat writer for the *Bulletin,* joked that they would make a movie about my life someday. When we went on the road we were playing so poorly that I was the marquee attraction for every newspaperman and TV reporter. I was an anomaly, so much so that, during our first visit to Los Angeles, Jim Murray wanted to interview me. He was up there

with Red Smith and Grantland Rice as the greatest sports-
writers who ever lived, and he wanted to sit down with me. I
was the most sought-after Eagle for speeches throughout
Philadelphia and my confidence grew tremendously, even
while I asked myself: Do I deserve it?

One afternoon I sat down with Dick Coury. I was concerned, I didn't want there to be resentment from my teammates, like there had been during training camp. We had
people like Bill Bergey, who was a four-time Pro Bowler, and
Roman Gabriel and John Bunting, big-time guys. If I lost
them in the locker room it wouldn't matter how many special-
teams tackles I made, they'd see me only as a glory hound.
But Coury was so wise, he calmed me down and told me to be
grateful, to be patient, to be honest, and to be thankful that
anyone had an interest in me at all. People would tell me I
was courageous and I'd laugh them off. Courageous to me was
the baton twirler from Interboro who was critically burned
when her flaming baton caught her dress on fire. Courageous
to me was the guy who worked as a locker room attendant for
the Eagles and was partially paralyzed by a stroke. On days
when I needed treatment for my shoulder or my hamstring
and could barely move it would be easy to get down. Then I'd
see him struggling to walk and realized I had it easy.

But nothing put my aches and pain in perspective like doing work with Eagles Fly for Leukemia. Shortly after the season began I was asked to attend some fund-raisers for Eagles
Fly. Several years earlier, Eagles tight end Fred Hill learned
his daughter Kim had the disease. At the time, she was given

a 1 percent chance to live for the next six months. Hill's teammates and Leonard Tose made it their mission to help the family. They held fund-raising dinners and made individual contributions. They organized a fashion show and collected donations at a home game, which raised $20,000. Soon after pledging their support, the Eagles presented the Children's Hospital in Philadelphia with a check for $125,000. As Kim successfully fought the disease, Tose decided to make Eagles Fly for Leukemia the team's official charity. He was such a legendary spender and the stories of his big tips and bigger gambles were what made the headlines. But Tose also personally covered the expenses for every Eagles Fly for Leukemia event, so all the money raised went directly to research. (Soon after that first donation, Eagles GM Jim Murray had an idea: He approached McDonald's about creating a green milkshake for St. Patrick's Day. He said they should call it a Shamrock Shake, and all the proceeds should go toward a house where parents could stay while their children were receiving treatment. In 1974, Tose and Murray would open the first Ronald McDonald House, in Philadelphia.)

The first couple of Eagles Fly events I went to didn't impact me that much. Then I visited the kids at Children's Hospital. I was scared. And I felt guilty that I was so healthy and all these kids who were critically ill were smiling at me like I was something special. I went back every Monday during the season with Denny Franks, Richie Osborne, and Spike Jones. I stopped being scared because those kids were so cheerful and courageous, it was incredibly uplifting.

I didn't think I needed a reality check of how good I had it. But those visits were always in the back of my mind. When game day came, no matter how bad we were losing, my enthusiasm could not be contained. I was a whirling dervish on the sidelines, constantly jumping up and down on the balls of my feet when I wasn't in the game. I just couldn't sit still. Bill Bergey used to joke about how much it bugged him; he teased me that anyone my age starting an NFL career and acting like that was a little dopey. When we scored, I was the first guy on the field to celebrate. This was all just a game to me, win or lose. It sure beat the alternatives. Midway through the season we played the Raiders, who would go on to win the Super Bowl that year, and one of their players told me I was a marked man. I couldn't believe it, I was so thrilled. Me, the old man, being marked by a team good enough to win the Super Bowl.

I had constant reminders of the company I now kept and where I had come from. Every week Vermeil invited a different group of players over to his house for dinner. He'd cook up tremendous steaks and serve the finest wines from Napa Valley. The rule was that you could not talk about the Eagles at all. If you talked about sports or your days as an athlete it had to be stories from college or high school or Pee Wee. I'd be at the table and hear our tight end Charlie Young talking about being at USC and playing UCLA. Meanwhile, all I had were stories about DelCo touch football and hanging out at Max's Tavern afterward.

There's a difference between being positive and believing

you can win. And Vermeil did his best to make sure we did the latter. That wasn't easy, since we went on a three-game losing streak in October, a month that ended with the Eagles playing at the Giants on Halloween. Fortunately, the Giants were in worse shape than we were. By the end of October they were 0–7 and ranked near the bottom of the conference in nearly every statistical category. We were either getting the exact team we needed to end our losing streak, or we were about to catch a team just mad enough to embarrass us.

I used to love playing the Giants. Their stadium, the Meadowlands, in New Jersey, was brand-new and you could see the New York City skyline from there. It didn't matter to me how bad the team was, that was the biggest stage in the world. No place better to play than there. Our bench was practically in the stands and the fans would rank on us the entire game. They weren't nasty, not nearly as bad as fans in New England and Washington, but more playful. They acted like it was all part of the game, nothing personal. Since my story had become pretty well known at this point they had a good time coming after me for my age. They didn't know my teammates were more biting than they could ever be.

The first quarter of the game was tough to watch, even as a player. We missed a field goal, they went backward on one drive, and then we went backward on the next. Finally, midway through the second quarter, Larry Marshall made a big gain on a Giants punt and gave us the ball in Giants territory. Six plays later, we scored our first touchdown. Later in the quarter, after another good return by Larry, we scored with less than thirty seconds left in the half, giving us a 10–0 lead.

By the fourth quarter the Giants were pretty beaten down, but we hadn't been able to put them away. With a little more than nine minutes remaining, we needed a big play, the kind that would pin the Giants deep in their own territory and make them do something they hadn't done all game: Move the ball. From our own forty-four-yard line, Spike Jones punted the ball. I was lined up outside, as usual, and when I got down in my three-point stance I was shocked to see I was only being single-teamed. I had been disruptive the whole game—on a punt earlier in the second half I had tackled Jimmy Robinson for no gain—and those were against double teams. Against one guy I felt unstoppable. From my stance he had his fists at my eye level and he was waving them around and insulting me, my mother, my family, my past. Anything he could do to get in my head. I didn't pay attention. I just focused on making my first move. If I did that right, it was over for this guy. As soon as the ball was snapped I drove hard off my right foot, toward the sideline. It was just like playing wide receiver against a cornerback—if I got him moving outside and his hips turned, then I'd have the advantage. And that's exactly what happened. I jabbed hard one way, caught him leaning all the way, and then angled inside. He didn't even get a hand on me, and I had a free path all the way down to Jimmy Robinson.

He was standing on the ten-yard line, and Robinson was known for not wanting to make fair catches. I could see his blockers starting to set up their wedge, but it was too late to get in front of me because I had the angle that I needed to blow by them. As I ran, I caught sight of the ball in its path and then stared straight through Robinson's face mask at his eyes. I could see them getting bigger as the ball got closer, and I was timing my sprint to hit him at the exact moment the ball landed in his hands. He took one step forward to catch the ball and *bam!* I had left my feet and came across his body, putting my helmet squarely on the ball and my arms around his torso. We were completely locked up, which may be the only reason he held on to the ball. We both went flying to the turf, head over heels, a picture that was on the front page of the *Evening Bulletin*'s sports section the next day. Backed up deep in their own territory, the Giants went nowhere, and we won the game 10–0, the Eagles' first shutout in nearly ten seasons.

We had bused up the Jersey Turnpike the Saturday night before the game. The next morning all of the players' wives and girlfriends caravanned together and parked their cars in the Giants players' lot. Then, after the game, the two teams had a huge tailgate on a beautiful fall afternoon with our wives and girlfriends and a bunch of diehard Philly fans a lot of the players had gotten to know who called themselves the Green Machine. They were state police from Southern Jersey and after the party they arranged an escort all the way home.

I'm not sure what they would have done if we had lost.

WE PEAKED that Giants game. After that we lost five in a row, ending our skid the last game of the season, at home, against the expansion Seattle Seahawks. While I had made plenty of contributions on special teams, I had yet to catch a regular season pass. Vermeil told the newspapers he thought I deserved one, so near the end of the game, when the win was safely ours, he put me in. Twice he called my number, and both times the quarterback overthrew me. I didn't care. I knew I would have more chances the next year.

As elated as I was to have made the team, I was equally relieved when the season was over. Vermeil's practices were very long, and at the end of the season, in the cold, they were breaking all of us down. The shoulder I had injured during the preseason was still tight. I had pulled a hamstring that never healed. And nearly six months of standing, running, and jumping in cleats made the bottoms of my feet feel as if I were constantly walking on nails. I liked to think there was nobody on the team more energetic or committed than I, and by the end of the season even I needed a break. As soon as the Seattle game was over, Chuck Gardner drove me to my apartment, where I packed a bag and hopped a plane for Miami. When I got down there I sat on the beach and didn't move for a week.

I got back to Philly just before Christmas. I had a one-bedroom I had to pay for and a sleek Datsun that I owed money on, and it's not as though I were a big-time star making a six-figure salary. I needed to make some money during the off-season, and I assumed I'd go back to substituting when the schools reopened after Christmas.

At the time, *Rocky* had been in theaters for a month and had turned the character of an Italian underdog from Philly into a national icon. People couldn't get enough of the movie, seeing it five and six times, humming the theme song while they strolled down the street. Kids all over the country would watch the movie and then stage their own fake boxing matches, taking turns being Rocky. In Philly people were ecstatic because Rocky Balboa epitomized what everyone in the city saw in themselves: He was a street-smart guy with a heart of gold who would never give up. All he needed to achieve greatness was a chance to prove it. He was from the great fighting city of Philadelphia, a guy who dressed his dog in an Eagles jersey. People in town especially ate up the story of how Sylvester Stallone wrote the movie and forced producers to let him star in it, even when they wanted somebody else. The nerve of that guy, they thought. We wouldn't do it any other way, either.

This was also the year of the bicentennial, and in 120 minutes *Rocky* showed everything that was possible in the United States, that a guy could go from punching out deadbeat gamblers to fighting the world champ with a little bit of luck, grit, and opportunity. Between being celebrated as the birthplace of democracy and being featured in the movie, Philly was a city in full. It just swelled with pride.

I was a true-life version of Rocky. During that week I was away after the season ended, the Eagles kept getting requests for me to speak around the city. Pretty soon I was the most requested speaker in the history of the team. And they all wanted to pay me. At $150 a speech I could make more in fifteen or twenty minutes than I could in a week as a substitute teacher. Plus, I'd have more impact. People wanted to hear my story; I wanted to share it. I didn't think I was special, but I believed what I had done was special. I took risks, I quit my job, and I had lived my dream. And I wanted people to see that anything was possible.

Or maybe people were just curious to see if I was as crazy off of the field as I was on it. Maybe they thought I'd jump through some burning hoop. I think people were surprised when I blushed, stammered, and stuttered my way through those first few engagements.

Before my first speech I met with Vermeil for some public-speaking advice. He gave me a Nightingale tape, a motivational tape, and told me to buy the whole set. The tapes had little nuggets of wisdom, such as "Attitude is the key to success" and "Treat every person you meet like the most important person in the world." They were helpful, but then I decided to build my speeches around the sayings Vermeil had taped around the locker room, such as "No one ever drowned in sweat" and "The greatest reward is knowing that you did the best you could do," and, my favorite, "Opportunity is worth to a person exactly what their preparation enables them to make of it." I also used an oldie but a goodie from George Corner: "Happy are those who dream dreams and are willing to pay the price to make those dreams come true."

Mostly I was speaking to kids. It seemed like every Friday night and Sunday afternoon I was doing another Pee Wee football banquet. I did about 6 or 7 speeches a week, more than 150 during that off-season, and made close to $60,000. I tripled my salary talking about what I had done compared to what I made actually doing it. Jim Murray joked that I did more speeches in that off-season than the pope did in a lifetime. At one Italian banquet hall I spoke so often that they knew exactly when in my speech to start bringing out the Italian wedding soup. I became such a banquet regular I got offers from a lot of different clothiers, including Boyd's, to give me suits, but I picked up some cheap ones from the Bazaar of All Nations.

I grew sick of eating rubber chicken, but I never got tired of trying to make a connection with people. One night I drove seven hours to a city on the New York State border, played in a charity basketball game, then drove all through the night to walk twenty miles as chairman of a March of

Dimes benefit. I remembered when I was a kid and Tommy McDonald spoke at my football banquet and how much that resonated with me, so I always gave my all for every event—which wasn't always easy. I would get there and see what looked like five thousand trophies on the dais and know I was in for a long night if I didn't ask to go first. Even if I did, I'd be talking and see dads downing beers like they were bottles of water. There would be fifteen or twenty empty beer bottles at every table. I couldn't blame the dads; this was probably their one night out after working a tough week. But it didn't make it any easier to inspire when you've got to shout into the microphone to be heard over the chatter.

I was asked to speak at George Corner's football banquet. I didn't charge for that one. By this time he had moved on to become the head coach at Radnor, which was a real upscale high school near Villanova on the Main Line. I told those kids how much George meant to me and how he was responsible for putting me in the NFL. Some of them believed it, and I like to think it saved him some grief from kids who might have tried giving him a hard time.

Soon after that I gave a speech to the Glenolden Boys Club, for the kids in the football program my father had started more than twenty years earlier. I didn't charge for that one, either, even though they had me follow a dog show. It was at a firehouse, and it wasn't just full of kids who played football for the Boys Club, but teachers of mine from grammar school, kids I had grown up with and loved who were proud of me, kids I had grown up with who hated me and were envious (I can't lie and say I didn't mind seeing them, either), and parents of old friends. My making it on the Eagles meant as much to them as it did to my parents. Not just because I had made it as a pro football player. If it had been the Cleveland Browns or the San Francisco 49ers or the New England Patriots my journey wouldn't have been as spectacular. The fact it was the Eagles, that they could see me playing for the team we all loved for so long, is what mattered most. After the last game of the 1977 season a reporter asked me about the team and what I thought my prospects were for the next season. We had won our last game, and my response was, "I'm so happy, I don't care what position I play as long as I'm wearing an Eagles uniform." That's how I felt my entire career. Playing in the NFL but for another team would have fulfilled a fantasy, but it would not have been as sweet. Part of that was because of the people who were so close to me. I fulfilled all of their dreams lining up in Eagles green, not just mine.

Even my old coach with the Bell, Ron Waller, asked me to speak at a football camp he was giving in Washington, D.C. When I went down there a lot of my old teammates—King Corcoran, Claude Watts, and John Land—were there, too. And I felt for them. Their careers had been taken from them because a whole league couldn't make it. It was sad, actually. We were all around the same age, only I had gotten such a late start as a football player I hadn't been beaten down the way they were. They had played too long in semi-pro leagues, on

too many fields covered with rocks and bricks. Their bodies
had just taken so much more of a pounding than mine.

Of course, even while I was giving these you-can-do-it
speeches, I still always questioned whether or not I belonged.
I had been asked to speak at a fund-raiser in Lancaster along
with Vermeil, Brooks Robinson, and John Unitas. Vermeil invited me to drive with him and I was scared to death. Even after a season's worth of his coaching and support, I was still
intimidated by him. He was confident without being cocky;
he never seemed to be unsure of any decision he made or any
word that he said. Whether he was standing in front of a
room full of rabid fans, a banquet hall filled with Philly's
finest businessmen, or a locker room packed with players who
were beaten up and couldn't stand the sight of him, he had
the same steady command of his voice.

Lancaster was a ninety-minute drive from Philly and I didn't
know what we were going to talk about. I just knew I wouldn't
start the conversation. And Vermeil didn't make me. He
started talking about the event and how great it was to be on
the dais with Brooks Robinson and Johnny U. I mentioned
that I didn't understand why the organizers of fund-raisers
wanted me to speak. I didn't feel as if I carried the same weight
as the other celebrity athletes. I hadn't won a World Series like
Brooks or an NFL championship like Unitas. I hadn't even
caught an NFL pass. I was half-joking when I said it, but Vermeil turned so serious I thought he would pull the car over. He
told me I had nothing to be ashamed of, that I deserved to be
on that dais more than anyone, that my road to the pros was

harder and I had achieved as much by making it as anyone had by winning championships. After that I was so fired up I'm surprised I didn't tackle Johnny U. before we sat down.

Vermeil proved he wasn't just blowing smoke my way that February, when he signed me to three one-year deals. I would earn $26,000 in 1977, $35,000 in 1978, and $45,000 in 1979. None of the deals were guaranteed until I made the team. But the gesture, which meant that Vermeil and Jim Murray wanted to make me a part of their plans, was overwhelming. I signed the deals five days before I turned thirty-one. I walked out of the stadium with those new contracts under my arm and I was on cloud nine, like a kid who is told he would eat nothing but ice cream and candy for the next three years.

The first thing I did was buy a bottle of champagne. Then I headed to my parents' house, where I was going to change my clothes for a speaking engagement later that evening. As I was driving, tears started rolling down my face. It just hit me that I wasn't a fluke. People always asked me if I could put it in perspective and I just never could. I still can't.

A few days after signing the deals, I celebrated my thirty-first birthday by going for a jog around the slush-covered streets of South Philly. I liked the atmosphere in this part of town, it gave me a chance to get out among people like me. No matter how cold and gray it was, I always got a warm feeling on those jogs because of the way people identified with me. Two years earlier I was one of them, in the upper deck, feeling the disappointment when the Eagles lost. Because of Vermeil, we all felt we were building toward a Super Bowl. It sounded silly since we had just finished the season 4–10, but we believed. Especially after the Eagles traded for a young quarterback named Ron Jaworski that March. Jaws was a rifle-armed four-year vet who had played in college at Youngstown State and been a second-round pick of the Rams. But the Rams were loaded at quarterback and he rarely got a chance to play in L.A.—he started just nine games there (although one of them was a playoff win). When he turned down a contract extension from the Rams, they happily let us take him off of their hands. We got a steal. Jaws was talented enough to throw with any quarterback in the league and still young enough to get better. But, most important, he wanted to learn. He'd become antsy sitting for the Rams and when Vermeil got him it was as though he had a new life. From the beginning, Vermeil made it clear that Jaworski was going to be his guy at quarterback, no matter how much the Eagles lost or fans booed. Vermeil saw something in Jaworski that made him a believer, and the player in turn believed in the coach.

He was the perfect Philly quarterback: not too flashy, not too pretty, the kind of guy who enjoyed going out for beers with his offensive linemen. He was just a kid from the steel-mill town of Lackawanna, New York, who was hard and tough and fearless. After high school, he was drafted by the St. Louis Cardinals and desperately wanted to play in the minor leagues. But his father, who worked in a lumberyard, pushed him to go play football in college. When Jaws balked, his dad made him go spend part of the summer working in the steel mills, so he could see what life would be like if baseball didn't work out. After two weeks, Jaws committed to playing football at Youngstown State.

We liked Jaws because he had his priorities in order. One of the reasons he chose Youngstown State, despite getting offers from bigger schools, was so his parents could drive the three and a half hours to his games. He always believed he could throw the ball through defenders. But with Vermeil he learned how to read defenses and throw with touch and really become an NFL quarterback. He spent almost as much time in the film room as Vermeil did.

In fact, the first time Jaworski saw me was while watching film shortly after he was traded. I was so intense on special teams and so enthusiastic on the sidelines he wondered what I was on. Vermeil just shook his head and said, "Nothing. That's just Vince."

Although, when we actually met, I didn't exactly make him think I was sane. It was in April and we were at the Vet working out. The Phillies had played the day before and the grounds crew that had cleaned up left a bunch of empty trash bags lying around. It had rained pretty hard that morning, so Denny and I took trash bags, punched out some holes for our arms and heads and threw them on like a poncho. Then I sprinted as fast as I could for about twenty-five yards toward the outfield and did a full-on, face-first dive. I must have slid another twenty-five yards, with water spraying behind me like a wake on a lake. I got up and, naturally, I was soaked. Jaws was speechless. He just thought I was nuts.

But he wasn't a prima donna, and that helped bring the team together. That first day he worked out with us we were running 110-yard sprints. Vermeil had been bragging to the newspapers that he was so excited about his team because of how hard they worked. The Eagles' trainers had tailored off-season conditioning programs for every guy on the roster, and Vermeil was convinced I was the best-conditioned athlete in America. At least that is what he kept telling me and anyone else who would listen. But Jaws tried to keep up anyway. We ran twenty-four 110-yard sprints, doing ten, then resting for five minutes, then doing eight, then resting five more minutes, then doing six. After just a couple my legs started to shake. And after ten my lungs were burning so hot I could barely breathe. I looked at Jaws and thought he was going to try to rescind the trade. But he never complained. He just hung with us the entire time.

Vermeil was right about several things during my tenure with the Eagles, including the comment that I may have been the best-conditioned athlete in America. I was fiercely dedicated. I knew how bad training camp had been the season before and wanted to suffer as little as possible. Denny Franks and I actually showed up to the Vet on January 2, 1977, to work out. Vermeil was there, working of course, but he kicked us out and told us the workout room was going to be closed until February 1. Sandy and I got married that June—Chuck Gardner was my best man—and two days after my wedding I was at the facility working out. Vermeil saw me, told me I was out of my mind, and kicked me out of the gym, again. When I went on my honeymoon I still worked out twice a day, running on the beach in the morning and jogging for a second time at night.

A lot of players who didn't stay in Philly during the off-season were given incentives in their contracts to stick around and work out under the team's supervision. I didn't get any training bonuses, but it didn't make me want to work out any less. I had a lot of goals for that off-season. Vermeil had a chart on the wall of the workout room at the Vet that kept track of who showed, how often, and how many miles they ran that day. I wanted to make sure I went into training camp at the top of that list. I also began the off-season benching 180 pounds, which was 15 pounds less than I weighed, and I wanted to finish it by benching 300 pounds. I got to 296. I was at the Vet every day, Monday through Friday, from nine in the morning until noon.

On the days that I jogged through the streets I would get a lot of "Yo, Vinnie" and "Hey, Italian Stallion," or "Go get 'em, Rocky." Whenever I saw the Vet I'd think to myself, God-damn, that is where I work. I make my living as a professional football player. I didn't need a workout bonus to get there every morning, I just needed that view. Then I would finish my jog in a full-on sprint into the stadium and toward the locker rooms. The routine was always the same every day: work out, eat lunch, relax, give a speech. It was a great lifestyle.

JIM MURRAY WAS a fantastic marketing man. A Villanova grad, he had worked as the school's sports information director before joining the Eagles in 1969 as a public relations assistant. He was about as decent a man as any who was living in Philadelphia, which is probably why Leonard Tose named him the Eagles' GM, even though Jim had never played or coached football before. Everyone in Philly was stunned when Tose promoted Jim from a front office administrator to the boss. Murray was from West Philly and turned the organization into something that symbolized more than losing in the city. Eagles Fly for Leukemia, which Murray administered, set the standard for team-run charities in professional sports and helped the franchise connect with fans in a positive way, even when there was nothing to cheer for on the field. Ray Didinger wrote in his book *The Eagles Encyclopedia* that Tose trusted Murray so implicitly that the Eagles' owner had actually written a clause into his will that Murray would take over the team if Tose died while he still owned the franchise.

While Jim didn't necessarily know a trap play from a screen play, he did know how to spot talent. He was the one who traded for the madman linebacker Bill Bergey and the guy we called the Polish Rifle, Ron Jaworski. He was the one who sealed the deal that convinced Vermeil that Philly was worth leaving California for.

And he also knew, more than anything, how to sell sports. While the Eagles were showing improvement and gaining momentum after that 1976 season, thanks to Vermeil's twenty-four-hours-a-day, seven-days-a-week work schedule, we still weren't going to draw people in because of our play. Murray had to take advantage of what he had in front of him. And I was right there, ready and willing to help.

The *Rocky* phenomenon had so completely taken hold of the country that, while I at first bristled at the idea of being compared to some fictional character, I eventually just accepted it and dove right in. My agent even printed up T-shirts that had my picture on them with the words PHILLY'S OWN ROCKY above it. I didn't love that idea. But I went with it. We were trying to promote the Eagles, and me, too.

The most famous scene in *Rocky II* is when Sylvester Stallone runs through the streets of South Philly, picking up jogging partners along the way. Pretty soon it seems like half of Philadelphia is running alongside him, cheering him on. Toward the end of the run he sprints ahead of everyone and bounds up the steps of the Philadelphia Museum of Art, two at a time, until he reaches the top. When he gets there he's jumping up and down with his hands raised high in the air, and all the fans who had been jogging behind him finally catch up and bounce up and down with him. He was like the pied piper of South Philly. Apart from the regular "Go get 'em, Vince," I never had any fans chase me down and root for me as I ran through the streets. I'd pass the playgrounds, the old men playing bocce ball, the guys on the corner singing around the garbage can, and none of them ever stopped what they were doing and joined me in a sprint through Philly. And I never ended my runs with a sprint up the steps of the art museum.

Until Jim Murray told me I should. When NFL Films came around during the off-season to get footage of me for a television segment, they asked me to run up the steps. *Sports Illustrated* visited Philly for a story that would run during the season. Under the headline "Recovering from a Rocky Start," they asked me to pose at the top of the steps. I was holding a football, wearing a WHO'S NUTS? T-shirt, and had the city of Philly at my feet.

ELEVEN

WAS ANXIOUS to begin my second season. I had had
enough of banquets and accolades. I wanted to play football
for the Eagles, get back to doing what I loved most. Vermeil
had written every veteran early in the summer and asked if
they would report to camp three days earlier than they originally planned. But that wasn't early enough for me. Rookies
always came to camp three or four days ahead of the vets, and
I wanted to be there when they arrived. I called Vermeil and
asked him if that would be all right. I was in great shape. The
Eagles had a computer program that measured increases in
strength, and my upper body was 125 percent stronger than
the season before. My overall strength had improved by 25
percent. I wanted to prove how much better I had become,
that I wasn't just a one-year wonder. Vermeil must have felt
how excited I was over the phone. He told me to relax, that

I would get plenty of time to make plays. Then he said the sweetest words I had ever heard: "Vince, you're a veteran now. You've worked hard enough. You deserve the extra week's rest."

An NFL veteran. Even with all that had happened—the speaking engagements, the photo shoots, the TV interviews— I still got chills just hearing those words. There were a couple of times during the off-season when I had to remind myself that I was no longer just a fan, that I didn't need to renew my season-ticket order. I was so pumped after hearing Vermeil call me an NFL veteran I hopped on my bike and rode around the neighborhood for more than two hours.

Because we had added Jaws and because Vermeil canvassed the state giving speeches during the off-season, always with the passion and conviction of a college coach trying to drum up support for his program, there was real enthusiasm when camp began. We didn't feel like a team that had won just four games the year before. Even though our talent was only nominally better than it had been, Vermeil had us believing we had no excuses for losing. And he used every means available for sending us messages about what he expected. When Roman Gabriel, a former NFL MVP, showed up to camp late Vermeil demoted him, fined him, threatened to make him take a pay cut, and discussed trading him. He sat Gabriel down and told him point-blank he wouldn't accept any disruptions if he were backing up Jaworski. And unlike most coaches, when reporters asked him about Gabriel's status, Vermeil didn't blanch or try to sidestep the issue. "If Gabe reported when he was supposed to," Vermeil told the *Delaware County Daily Times,* "he'd be my number one quarterback."

Vermeil had a square jaw that jutted out even further when he spoke. Just looking at his face and hearing the passion in his voice made us want to run through the wall and hit someone. We were, he reminded us, the best-conditioned, hardest-working football players in the NFL. No one in Dallas or New York would do more with less than we would; we had no excuse for not being in every game. True or not, we were sold.

Vermeil had done a good job shedding the dead weight from the team the season before. And he didn't just bring in players off the street to make lines long during the training-camp drills, so this camp would not be as physically difficult as it had been twelve months earlier. As opposed to bringing in 120 players, like he did in 1976, Vermeil brought in only about 85 guys. Not that camp was easy. It just no longer felt like torture. And a lot of the little things that made the Eagles feel unprofessional from the season before—broken projectors, broken screens, broken window shades in film rooms—had been fixed. Vermeil was upgrading the franchise in every possible way, turning us from a league joke into, if not a league power, a team other players didn't dread the idea of playing for. Which meant that what practices lacked in pure physical brutality, they made up for in competition and spirit. There were far fewer complaints from veterans than the year before. Far fewer guys looked at me funny—or wanted to knock me out cold—when I grabbed a practice pass and sprinted forty yards downfield for the end zone. My teammates had accepted me after that first season, and now watching me go full tilt on every play encouraged them, instead of just making them hate me. And, after the grousing he'd heard the previous summer, even Vermeil was stunned at how many of his veteran players reported to camp in shape. For him, that was vindication of his program and his efforts. Eagle practices were now filled with guys who had either bought into his the-only-way-to-kill-time-is-by-working-it-to-death system or were anxious to do so. Eagle effort was no longer just a team mantra, it was the way we played.

I was hoping to move up the depth chart and get more time as a wide receiver. I had gone that entire first year without catching a pass. During the off-season I worked hard on my timing with Jaws while running patterns at the Vet. Dick Coury was, as usual, encouraging, and Vermeil had talked about using more three-receiver sets, with me as the third wideout. I had already impressed the coaches with my enthusiasm and attitude and reckless disregard for my body on special teams. Now I had to be a precise route runner, show good concentration and sure and steady hands, and prove I could be a skill player, not just a kamikaze running down the sideline.

But I also knew I was going to make the team, whether it was as a receiver or just as a special teams ace. And with that came a sense of relief I had never felt during that first training camp. So now I didn't worry if I decided to take a day off here and there. Every veteran in every training camp knows how to get himself out of practice when he needs a break. You say you tweaked a hamstring or pulled a muscle in your back or strained your neck. It's always something harmless, something that never shows up on an X-ray, something that won't keep you out for very long and that a trainer can't refute you have. Coaches know you might just be giving yourself a day off, but if it's just that and nothing more, they let it slide and don't hold it against you. It's how veterans, especially older ones, pace themselves and keep themselves healthy during the dog days of training camp. You never meet an old veteran who isn't also wise. Those guys last because they know how to bend the rules.

Most coaches don't even bother making you suit up on your "sick" days. But Vermeil wasn't most coaches. Deciding you needed a day off from hitting never meant you got a day off from training. It meant you were the first ones up to get taped, even before the rookies. It meant you didn't get to nap after lunch, like those players going through two-a-days, because your body didn't need to recuperate as much. Depending on which injury you pretended to be suffering from, you either walked around the field during practice or rode the stationary bike. The entire time. With your helmet and pads on. Sometimes we would sweat so much just from walking around in circles that our pads doubled in weight, from ten to twenty pounds.

One afternoon John Bunting and I had decided to give ourselves a break from the hitting and take a spa day. By 1977 Bunting was already an Eagle legend for his determination and study habits. When he was a rookie in 1972, he was a long shot to make the team. The Eagles had drafted him in the tenth round out of North Carolina. Back in those days, the higher the jersey number they assigned you the less the coaches thought of you. John was assigned number 95. And he'd wear it his entire career. John was 220 pounds, and admittedly slow, but he made up for it with smarts. Perhaps only Vermeil studied more film. Players on defense joked that he might have known more about the Eagles scheme than the coaches who devised it and often found him giving them lessons after practice was over. Vermeil was no doubt impressed with Bunting's work ethic and his intelligence, because when Vermeil coached the Rams to the Super Bowl during the 1999 season, Bunting was his co-defensive coordinator.

Bunting and I walked around the field, our helmets and shoulder pads on. Our bodies baked underneath the sun. The rest of our teammates were trying to kill one another, but that seemed less monotonous than the duty we had consigned ourselves to. Bunting tried teaching me to chew tobacco. I swallowed some and wound up puking all over the field. We looked pretty ridiculous. Finally, Bunting just looked at me and said, "Man, we're a couple of shit heads, aren't we?" The next day we were back at practice.

Late that August, for our third preseason game, we hosted the Patriots. Preseason games usually don't mean much. But we were a team still struggling to define ourselves. Every game meant something because every game was a chance for us to prove we could win. The Patriots were a particularly good target because they had Super Bowl aspirations. And I was anxious to get back on the field with Tim Fox, the New

England safety who had leveled me with a cheap shot the year before. Some of the papers had actually played it up, writing about the two of us going after each other and Fox saying he was just trying to intimidate because that was part of the game.

The night before the game I had a dream, which was odd because I never had dreams about football. I saw us winning the game 20–13 and afterward I went into the locker room to celebrate with my teammates, but none of them were there. Only Vermeil was there, alone, waiting for me. He told me all the guys were up in the pool. I didn't know how the points were scored or where the pool was. All I knew was that we won 20–13 and Vermeil had waited in the locker room to celebrate with me. I told Larry Marshall about the dream and he looked at me the same way as when we first met—like he was thinking, This guy is still crazy. Then he said, "Now you know why we aren't roommates on the road anymore."

Of course, we began the game down 10–0, and it didn't look like my dream was going to come true. But I was trying hard to make it happen. In the second quarter Spike Jones lofted a high-arching punt toward the Patriots' goal line. It was a special-teams play that we practice on short punts, where he gets as much hang-time as possible and I race down ahead of the ball, turn my back to the goal line, and field it as though I'm returning the punt, downing it inside the five-yard line. But I was double-teamed on this play. I had to fight through the middle of the defenders while keeping my eye on the punt, which was sailing high above my head. I dipped low to get some leverage and found a crack between the two Patriots' hips, and then began sprinting hard down the sideline. There was no way I would pass the ball and get in position to field it as we had practiced. I could only hope to be close and get a good bounce. The ball hit the ground as I crossed the five-yard line. I couldn't believe my good luck. Seven times out of ten a ball coming straight down like that careens into the end zone. As I neared the goal line and the ball came back down to earth, I knew I wouldn't be able to stop my forward momentum. While still moving I cradled the ball and tossed it around my back and out of bounds. The Patriots would start their next drive inside their own one-yard line.

Later that quarter, after another punt, I nailed the Pats' All-Pro punt-returner Stanley Morgan, only to have the play wiped out by a penalty. We had to kick again. Replaying a special-teams down is one of the most taxing experiences in the NFL. After one fifty-yard sprint while fighting off double teams your legs shake and your lungs burn. To have to do it again right away invites problems for both teams. Even for players in top condition, there is the potential for a lapse in concentration. The end result is usually a penalty, a big play, or a catastrophic injury. This time I was single-covered off the snap and while I was exhausted, the guy who had to block me was even more tired. I raced past him and had my eyes locked on taking down Morgan again. As I got closer I felt a shove and a pull from behind and I went down to the turf. I had been held, a ten-yard penalty against the Pats, which was better than if I had hit Morgan myself.

At halftime we were losing 10–7 and Vermeil had seen enough of his starters. In the second half he started at quarterback a rookie out of Stanford, Mike Cordova, who had been our second pick in the eleventh round of the draft. He was fourth-string on the depth chart. In six weeks of practice he had been horrible. During seven-on-seven drills he was so inaccurate he actually overthrew the six-foot-eight Harold Carmichael. When Vermeil decided Cordova would get some playing time, we all just assumed it was so the coach could see him stink up a game and then cut the quarterback with a clear conscience.

Early in the third quarter Cordova got his chance. We had just picked off the Pats and Cordova led a nice drive down to New England's fourteen-yard line. But now it was tense: We were deep in Pats territory with a first down and a chance to take the lead. Preseason or not, nobody goes out there after weeks of training to lose a game. In the second halves of preseason games especially, the tension is heightened because so many of the players on the field are second- and third-stringers trying to make the team. For those guys, every play might as well be the last play of the Super Bowl.

I was no different, since I was on the field along with Cordova. The call Vermeil sent in was a pass play, 673. Cordova had a hard time figuring out the hand signals and by the time he got to the line of scrimmage, the play clock was dwindling down. I was sure we'd get hit with a penalty, but just as the clock hit zero, the center snapped the ball. The play was supposed to be a pass to our tight end in the right corner of the end zone. If he wasn't open, then Cordova was supposed to read through his options from right to left. I was what's called the "come late" guy, meaning if he didn't see anyone open as he scanned the end zone, I would be cutting across from left to right. I was the last option on the play.

As Cordova looked right, he didn't see anyone open. All along the right side of the field, everyone was covered. Coming from the other side I had gotten just a step on the defender, and I could see Cordova's eyes get big as he saw me coming into his line of sight. Only about twenty yards separated me from the quarterback, but Cordova let loose a pass hard enough to go on a straight line for fifty yards. The cornerback guarding me cut in front of my path and tipped the ball, but just barely. I never lost sight of it as I watched it hit my hands. I heard a loud snap and thought the laces were going to rip the palm of my hand. But I held on and tumbled to the turf. Cordova was holding his breath and when he saw me come down with it, he jumped two feet into the air.

This was my first NFL touchdown catch, and it was the go-ahead touchdown. I leaped up, threw the ball high, and raised my arms up in the air like Rocky on top of the art museum steps and then banged myself on my helmet to make sure I wasn't dreaming this, too. I had seen my dad in his seat at two o'clock that afternoon so I pointed in his direction and then tilted my head back toward the sky. With the biggest smile on my face, I closed my eyes and just tried to soak in the cheers from the Philly fans. Which is why I never saw my teammates heading toward me in a swarm from the sideline. The first guy to reach me was Larry Marshall. He lifted me up, began jumping up and down with me in his arms, and got so excited he actually flipped me over his shoulder pads. I landed headfirst on the turf, smashing my face into my face mask and opening a huge gash across the bridge of my nose. As things calmed down, I sat down on the bench on the sideline as teammates continued to come over and bang my shoulder pads with congratulations. Then I took a deep breath, exhaled, and, before I could hold back, I was crying tears of joy.

I had one more experience later that game that made me realize how far I'd come. It was another punt and, again, I had beaten my man down the field and was making a beeline for Morgan. As I slowed down to gather myself and make the hit I was whacked from behind, hard enough that my head was slammed against the ground and I felt a little woozy. I had been clipped, out of frustration on the part of the other player. He then stood over me for a second as if to boast that he'd gotten the last laugh in the game. Then I saw the ref behind him throw a flag. As I started to smile, his grin disappeared. Then, while pointing over his shoulder to the flag, I said, "I think the ref left you something." He turned around to scream at the ref and I strutted off the field. It would have been the perfect moment if I hadn't been so disoriented that I started to walk toward the wrong sideline before my teammates turned me around.

After the game, which we'd go on to win 21–10, Vermeil told reporters, "I've really become spoiled by the play of Vince Papale. I expect him to perform like this every game.

He works his butt off during practices and when he plays a game like this it seems only natural. He's the kind of player you know you have to keep around."

Just before our first game of the season it became clear to me Vermeil wasn't the only person who felt that way. We were opening at home against the Tampa Bay Buccaneers. They were in just their second season and had gone winless in their first year. It was one of the first times we had been picked to win a season opener in several years. And because we had played well during the preseason, we felt good about our chances for the regular season.

Even when we had home games the team stayed in a hotel on Saturday night. We'd have a team meal and then a final team meeting. Before the Tampa game Vermeil went over the basics of our game plan and then told us who our team captains would be for the year. The coaches had nothing to do with choosing captains; they were voted for by the players. First, he announced Harold Carmichael's name as the offensive leader. This was nothing we hadn't expected. Then he said Bill Bergey had been voted defensive captain. Naturally, I thought, since he had become a perennial Pro Bowler. As he began to name the special-teams captain I assumed it would be Denny Franks, because that's who I had voted for. Instead, he said, "Special-teams captain, by a near unanimous vote, Vince Papale." I erupted, jumping from my seat, yelling, "Holy shit!" as I hugged Denny. As soon as the meeting ended I walked into the hotel lobby, found a pay phone, and called my dad to give him the news.

Then, the next day, with five minutes remaining in the first half of the game, on a third and twenty from our own thirty-five-yard line, I caught a fifteen-yard pass from Roman Gabriel, who was filling in for an injured Ron Jaworski. It was my first NFL catch during a regular season game and the last completion of Gabriel's sixteen-year career.

TWELVE

EAR THE end of the 1977 season, another sub-.500 year for the Eagles, I was a guest on *The Mike Douglas Show*. It was a fun interview and I must have done pretty well because, after the season was over, I got a call from the general manager of Philly's CBS affiliate. He had seen me on the show and asked if I'd be interested in doing some broadcasting during the off-season. I may have been a dreamer, but I knew one day I'd wake up and football would be over. I'd need another job eventually, and being a sportscaster seemed like a pretty good gig to fall back on.

I signed on as a weekend anchor at first. And I was as coachable as I had been when I first started playing with the Eagles. I learned how to write for TV and how to edit my own pieces and how to read highlights. It felt natural. I had grown comfortable speaking in front of large crowds, and I wasn't doing anything I didn't do already: talking about Philly's sports teams. Just because I was a pro didn't mean I still didn't root for the Flyers, Sixers, and Phillies as hard as I did before.

As the off-season wore on I started to pick up more responsibilities at the station, getting opportunities to do the sports on the evening telecasts at 5:30 and 11:00 during the week. I was taking the job more seriously, even scheduling an appointment to work with a TV coach who had tutored some of the network reporters. I was being paid only as a day-to-day freelancer, but my attitude was the same as it was when I made the Eagles: I'd prove how valuable I was first, and then I'd get a raise and security. It was a mutually beneficial relationship because their ratings improved as I laid the foundation for my life after football.

Not that I was ready to quit playing. Part of my deal with the station was that I would leave during training camp, and if things didn't work out with the Eagles, I'd be welcome back. As soon as I got to camp, I was glad I had a safety net. I worked just as hard as ever, but the reality was that the Eagles were getting better. Vermeil was following the exact blueprint he had drawn up in 1976. First, he wanted players who would lay it on the line and blindly follow his system. That would be the foundation of his team, then he'd get the talent he needed to win. Well, it was time to bring in the talent. I wasn't deluding myself. I had caught only one pass in two seasons; I knew that my role was on special teams and that if Vermeil wanted a player he trusted to play receiver and special teams, I'd be done.

I could see the receivers around me were younger, had better hands, and moved faster. Pretty soon I had fallen behind on the depth chart. I had a back injury that I didn't tell anyone about for fear of being cut on the spot. But it caused sciatica, and I was constantly losing feeling in my leg. I'd be trying to make a cut in practice, feel my leg go numb, and fall, making me unable to finish a route. During one preseason game against Atlanta I ran a curl route and just collapsed on the turf as the ball came my way. It sailed over my head. For the first time in two years, I looked my age on the field.

I did have my moments. We played the Dolphins in the Hall of Fame game and I scored a touchdown. But even those good plays were overshadowed by what the younger players I was battling did. In that Dolphins game, my touchdown couldn't compare to a dazzling punt return by a second-year player named Wally Henry that clinched the game. Even Bill Bergey called it "one of the most beautiful plays I've ever seen."

I hung on until the end of August. The night before Vermeil cut me I knew it was coming and Denny, my training-camp roommate, went out to buy us a few beers. We stayed up late watching TV and listening to music. Then I tossed and turned. I finally fell asleep only to wake up in a fright at one A.M. At exactly 6:45 the next morning, I heard a set of knuckles rapping on the door. I looked at Denny and he looked at me. It was assistant coach Bill Davis. Every player who has ever played in the NFL knows which coaches double as the grim reaper, the turk, and on the Eagles, Davis was that guy.

Denny and I secretly hoped Davis would say the other guy's name. But I knew better. As soon as I opened the door I said, "It's me." He said, "Report to Dick Vermeil." It was so official and cold the way he said it, as if he had never seen me before. But maybe that was how he dealt with telling so many guys it was time to wake up, the dream was over. I even tried to lighten the mood and said to him, "It's not good news, is it?" But he didn't answer.

When I got to Vermeil's room he had tears in his eyes. He tried to tell me how difficult the decision had been. That they had been up until one o'clock in the morning—the moment I had woken up—before finally settling on cutting me. Then he told me why he was letting me go. There were younger receivers on the squad who could play special teams and could develop into starters one day, too. Meanwhile, my body wasn't giving back what it should compared to the work I put in. But I didn't need the explanation, and I didn't hear much of it, either. My arms and legs were tingling and shaking. My chest was tied in a knot and I could hardly breathe. I had always dreaded hearing what I was hearing, and no matter how much I had imagined this scene, there was no way to prepare for it. I asked Vermeil if there was anything else I could have done to make it. He was in disbelief. He just laughed and said, "Yeah, you could have died on the field."

After I left Vermeil's room I had to walk back to my room and clean out my stuff. I didn't want to see anyone. The thought of saying good-bye to veterans I had cheered for, such as Harold Carmichael and John Bunting, was overwhelming.

I passed the dining hall where a lot of players were having breakfast and they all just stood in silence as I passed. It felt like I was some leader who had been assassinated and they were paying respects to my hearse as it passed by. No one said a word. But Vermeil would tell reporters later that day that he had never seen so many players and coaches with tears in their eyes once practice began.

I got back to my room and Denny was there. He was crying. Then I started crying. And we just stood there, both of us crying and shaking like a couple of babies.

As I carried my stuff to my car I saw Bill Davis. Now that the deed had been done he looked at me like the friends that we were. As we were trading good-byes a kid wearing an Eagles helmet came up to me and asked me for my autograph. Bill laughed and said, "Well, life goes on." I knew he was right. But when I got my car packed up all I could do was grip the steering wheel, stare at the practice field, and cry some more.

FOR THE NEXT week, I sat at home and, at least once a day, the phone rang. It would be Coach Vermeil, calling to see how I was feeling. He seemed to feel worse about having to cut me than I did about being cut. Finally I had to say, "Dick, stop calling me. Every time you do I think you're going to say you're bringing me back and I don't think I can take it."

It was only after he finally stopped calling, when I knew the Eagles wouldn't be taking me back before the season, that

I went back to Channel 10. Only the station didn't want me to just do weekends and fill-in work anymore. It wanted me to be the new sports director, doing twice-nightly newscasts. I was fired up and relieved at the same time. I had just built a house that I needed to pay for and I didn't have the NFL salary—and didn't expect the lucrative speaking engagements—anymore. Doing TV was a perfect transition. I agreed to take the job and began negotiating a contract with the station.

Those first couple weeks were tough. I had to cover the Eagles' home opener and when I walked into the stadium I saw signs that read BRING BACK PAPALE and PAPALE'S PAISANOS. I watched the game from behind the Eagles bench and had a hard time disassociating myself from the team. I wanted to run onto the field and congratulate guys when they did well and scream when I thought we had been cheated by the refs.

Meanwhile, the contract discussions with Channel 10 dragged on for several weeks, making the transition even more difficult. I wanted to be paid equal to the number-one sports guys at the other channels in Philly, and the station GM wanted to keep me at a low scale because of my inexperience. I kept doing the nightly newscasts at 5:30 and 11:00 P.M., assuming the deal would eventually get resolved. Then, one Monday in mid-September, three weeks into the Eagles' season, I was giving a speech to radio and television professionals at a luncheon in Philly. The Eagles had beaten the Saints the day before, but Wally Henry, who had replaced me, was lost for the season with a broken leg. Jim Murray was at the lunch and, after my talk about transitioning from pro football into television, he asked me if I was still in shape. I thought he was kidding at first and smiled, ready to joke around with him. But he asked again, "Seriously, are you in shape?" I answered, "Hell, yeah."

One of my neighbors was Doug Collins, the Sixers guard who eventually became a great NBA coach and broadcaster. He was rehabbing an injury at the time and kept coming over to get me out of the house and to work out with him. For a month I had been training as if I were still playing, only because Doug was pushing so hard to get himself ready for the NBA season. Not only was I in great shape, I was completely refreshed from not being hit for a month. My back had stopped hurting and the little strains from training camp had healed.

"Good," Murray said. "Because I think we might want to bring you back. Are you interested?"

I actually had to think about it for a second. I wondered what my future held. Even if I played one more season, that was probably it for me. But I could do TV for the rest of my life, I thought to myself. And the job I was being offered might not be around in a year. I told Jim, "I don't know if I want to come back, because we are trying to work out this TV thing here. I'll need to talk to my agent, but only if you think this is something that will really happen."

"Yeah, if you want it to happen, it will happen. But we need to know quick so we can move on if you're not on board."

Of course I wanted to play again, TV job or no TV job. So I

called my agent after the lunch and told him to let the station know it had until the end of the day to make me a fair offer or I was going back to the Eagles. They called back with nothing, telling me they couldn't make things happen that quickly. I was in the newsroom, getting ready for the 5:30 show. Just before I went on Jim Murray called me and asked what I was doing after the show. I told him I'd probably grab a bite and then he said, "Come eat down at the Vet, so you can sign your new contract with the Philadelphia Eagles." I practically jumped out of my seat with excitement, but I didn't tell any of the other reporters or producers. Not that they couldn't tell something was up. I went on the air at 5:30 and had so much enthusiasm one of the anchors, Larry Kane, said to me, "You'd think you were playing for the Eagles again."

The next morning he—and the rest of Philadelphia— would read a headline in the newspaper that proclaimed: "Rocky II: Eagles to Sign Vince Papale."

I DID ONE more interview for Channel 10 before rejoining the team. It was with myself. I went to the Vet dressed in my suit and stood in front of a camera asking questions. Then I went into the locker room, changed into my uniform, and answered them. With some fancy editing, I was able to get the first interview with Vince Papale after his return to the team.

Walking onto the field at JFK for that first practice back was an amazing feeling. It was a gorgeous fall day. Monsignor

Sharkey, the team pastor, came over to me, gave me a handshake and a hug, and told me I was important to the fabric and soul of the team. My teammates embraced me and immediately it felt as though I had never left. Then, that night, Denny and I went out and had as much fun bouncing around the bars as two guys can legally have.

Our season hadn't started out well. Before beating the Saints we lost our first two games—to the Rams and the Redskins—two elite teams in the league. They were the kind of games a team that is hoping to prove it has turned things around needs to win. Our fourth game of the season, and my first game back, was going to be at home against the Dolphins. Coached by Don Shula, who'd go on to win more games in NFL history than any coach, they were 2–1 and an annual Super Bowl contender, and favored to beat us by three points.

I was anxious when I got to the team hotel Saturday afternoon, a feeling that lasted all night. I watched a late movie on TV. Then I flipped over to *Saturday Night Live* before finally falling asleep. I woke up at 3 A.M. to the sound of TV static filling the hotel room. I got up for good at 7:30 and Denny and I drove over to the game in his smooth-looking Continental Mark IV. We didn't say a word on the drive over. Our chemistry was the same as it had always been. We snaked past city hall, drove through the Italian market, and eventually entered the Veteran's Stadium parking lot. We put on our pads, our uniforms, then our shoes, and sat on our stools, our legs bouncing and our bodies shaking as they had for so many games before. Then Vermeil walked into the locker room and said, "Okay special teams, let's go."

It's common for the offensive or defensive starting lineups to be announced before the game. Sometimes, when their heroes are being introduced, that's when the fans' energy is at its peak. No one ever introduced the special teams, because fans usually didn't know who any of us were. But that wasn't the case in Philly. Vermeil had seen the headlines my return had generated. And he knew his team needed an emotional boost to start the game. So, for the first time in NFL history, a special-teams unit was introduced over the loudspeaker. After the game Vermeil would admit he did it to get the fans riled up. "I wanted Vince's name announced," he said, "so they could show their appreciation."

Mine was the last name announced, and I shot out of that tunnel as though I had rockets attached to my cleats. I did what I always did when running onto the field for the first time before a game: sprinted toward the opposite end zone and pointed to the top of the stadium, where my dad and my friends were sitting. The Dolphins never had a chance that day—we beat them 17–3.

That game gave us the confidence boost that we needed. Before we could prove we were a team on the rise to the rest of the league, we had to prove it to ourselves. And beating the Dolphins did that for us. The next week we beat the Colts by a field goal in Baltimore and headed into the midpoint of the season with a .500 record for the first time in four seasons.

Our seventh game that year was against the Redskins. They had a new coach, Jack Pardee, whose wild offensive theories had turned his team into a scoring powerhouse. They had beaten us in a 35–30 shootout in Washington the second game of the year, and they had yet to lose a game all season. They had a gutsy quarterback in Joe Theismann and a bull of a running back in John Riggins. Unlike most high-scoring teams, the Redskins weren't dominated by finesse players who were afraid of contact. We thought they were a good match-up for us and we expected the game to be physical, especially since we were playing in front of our own fans.

And it was. Every time he snapped the ball Jaworski could hear the pads popping as our offensive linemen moved the Redskins off the line of scrimmage. "Bang! Crash! Just beautiful," Jaws told the *Evening Bulletin*. At the end of the first half we had a 10–3 lead and all the players were already exhausted. Both teams knew chances in the second half to get into the end zone would be few and far between, so we both had to seize every opportunity. In the third quarter, the Redskins lined up for a field goal from the two-yard line but instead went for a fake. Theismann was the holder, and our All-Pro defensive end Carl Hairston heard him yell, "Score," just as the ball was snapped. Hairston knew this was a fake, yelled, "Fake, fake," to the rest of the guys on the defensive line, and snuffed out the play.

The Redskins would tie the score 10–10 later in the game, but only after intercepting Jaws and setting themselves up close to the goal line. On the ensuing kickoff our return man took the ball from our three to the forty-seven-yard line. It's moments like these, late in a physical game, when all the two-a-days in pads for three hours at a time pay off. We weren't fresh, but we were battle tested. Spending the day beating the tar out of one another was something we had been doing since July. We could sense the Redskins were more fatigued. Vermeil then called four straight running plays, and our offensive line kept pushing back the Redskins defense until, finally, they had no more room to give, and we took a 17–10 lead.

We still didn't feel as if our lead was safe. We had just signed a new punter, Mike Michel, who had been on the team for less than twenty-four hours. He hadn't even kicked in a game since trying out for the Dolphins in the preseason. And Mike was not having a very good day. His first punt was fine. But on his second try he dropped the long snap from Denny and then had to hurry a kick to beat the rush. That punt went only ten yards. Which actually looked like All-Pro caliber stuff compared to his next punt. Knowing he was going to face a big rush, Mike got anxious. As he dropped the ball toward his foot he lost focus and . . . whiffed. He just flat-out missed the ball. I had never seen that in a professional game. None of us had. Amazingly, we didn't want to kill him. Maybe struggling all those years had made us more compassionate. But at halftime Denny took him aside and tried to console him. Then the special-teams leaders got together with the coaches and came up with new protection schemes for the second half so Mike wouldn't be so jittery. It was a close game, and we were convinced punting would be the difference between a win and a loss.

With two minutes left we faced a fourth down deep in our own territory, at the fifteen-yard line. All game, the fans and even some of the players had been waiting for the moment when we reverted back to being the same old Eagles, the team that finds a way to lose a game instead of fighting for a win. This should have been that moment. We were clinging to a one-touchdown lead, playing against an undefeated team with an explosive offense, punting from deep in our own territory, and relying on a kicker who kicked nothing but air earlier in the game. Given those circumstances, most knowledgeable Philly fans would have bet their last $100 that the Redskins would win this game.

As we lined up in the huddle, the Redskins called a time-out. They wanted to ice Mike, give him more time to think about the punts he had muffed during the game. I looked Mike in the eye and could see he was getting nervous. Everyone kept saying to him, "You can do it, you can do it." Finally I just told him to step away from the huddle. As I walked him back about five yards I said, "Visualize the way you kick in practice. That's all this is, a practice shot." I don't think he believed me. I know I didn't believe me. But I had to say something to get him away from the rest of us. He didn't need to hear what we were going to do to protect him, he just needed to kick the ball.

As I turned back to the huddle I noticed that all the coaches on Washington's sideline were yelling to their punt returner, Tony Green, "No fair catch, no fair catch." In our game with the Redskins earlier that season, Green had returned a punt eighty yards that proved to be the game-winning touchdown. So we were all wary of what he could do. But I thought it was odd they didn't want him to make a fair catch. We were punting from deep in our own territory. Green was standing at midfield. Even from there, with two minutes left and Washington's explosive offense, there would be plenty of time to score the game-tying touchdown.

We were all staying in to block. Instead of lining up wide like I usually did, I was in a three-point stance close to the line. All we cared about was keeping Mike protected and letting him be comfortable enough to get the ball off. I had two guys on top of me. But as I got into my stance I saw that their knuckles were red, not white, which is what they would be if they were going to attack. I thought I might be able to make one step to the outside, get them both off balance and moving that way, and then break downfield for the punter. Before the ball was snapped I screamed, "Zoro, zoro," which meant I was going to release off the line instead of staying in to block, so I'd need one of my teammates to cover the right edge by sliding right.

At the snap, I used one of my favorite moves as a receiver—an inside-out fake—that made the players assigned to block me turn their hips. Then Mike got off a booming, high-arcing forty-four-yard kick. I knew I had beaten my men. When I sprinted past I yelled, just a huge, primal scream, as if I were an old-time warrior running toward the enemy's front line.

One of the guys had been yapping all day about how he was going to break my jaw, like I was some kind of rookie who was going to be intimidated. That might have helped me get by him. If he had been quiet, who knows if I would have had that extra gear so late in the game.

It was windy in the Vet that day and the ball swirled back and forth as it reached the top of its arc. I could see as I raced down the field that it was just going to be me and Green, one-on-one. With the ball swerving around and me bearing down I expected him to call for a fair catch, despite the instructions from his coaches. But he didn't. I heard the crowd screaming as I got closer and as soon as the ball hit his hands, I tore into him. I could hear the breath escaping from his lungs and felt his body collapse around my shoulder pad. I saw the ball pop loose as soon as I hit him. One of my teammates picked it up. And, as we piled on top of him to celebrate, we all knew the game would be ours. Back on the sidelines Denny Franks and I embraced. A photographer was standing nearby and he snapped a picture, one that would win the Pro Football Hall of Fame's photo contest that year. The photographer caught the two us just as we were letting go, with one arm each still wrapped around the other's shoulder pads. Our helmets were dangling from our fingers at our hips and our heads were thrown back in pure joy. We were laughing—our mouths wide open—because we couldn't believe how far we had come and that we were in the middle of it all.

We weren't the same old Eagles anymore. By his third season as head coach Vermeil had filled his roster with enough guys like me who would outwork anyone, and enough playmakers like Jaworski, that we were a legitimate challenge to any team in the league on any given Sunday. After beating the Redskins we'd win four of our next six games, none by more than eight points, which proved how mentally tough we really were.

On the last day of the season we were playing at home against the Giants. It was a win-and-we're-in situation: If we won the game, we'd make the playoffs. It was brutally cold. The fans arrived with their faces covered in ski masks, carrying several blankets each and, no doubt, hiding flasks of blackberry brandy in their jackets. Before the game I was walking the field, trying to soak it all in. Having been lucky to be invited back on the team, I knew my time in the league was precious. If we lost, and this ended up being my last game, I wanted to remember how it looked and smelled and sounded. I wanted to remember how much the turf hurt when it was cold. If I was back in the stands again the next season, I didn't want to forget the sensation of having been on the field.

The diehards always arrived at the stadium early. As I walked around I saw Billy Thomas, who I used to share season tickets with and who I used to die with every Sunday. I gave him a wave and he waved back. One of the Eagles' assistant coaches saw me and when I turned around he said, "Today you are a far cry from being up in the stands, huh?"

The Giants never had a chance that day—we blew them out 20–3. But they still never let up. After one punt with about six minutes left I took a vicious shot while running downfield. I had a pretty bad headache when I walked off the field and needed to take a seat on the bench next to Denny. Then Jaworski came by. He was clapping his hands and screaming, "Only six more minutes and we're winners. We're winners." He was making everybody on the team get off the bench. And I forgot all about the pain. I looked at Denny and said, "Let's get up and be a part of this thing." We started yelling as loud as we could, as if we were fans in the 700-level of the Vet, and we didn't stop until the clocks on the giant scoreboard were lit up with zeroes.

When it was all over the players ran on the field. We circled the stadium and celebrated with the fans, shaking hands, slapping five, knowing it meant as much to them as it did to us. They were handing us beers, taking our pictures, standing in the cold for half an hour after the game to acknowledge what we had done. As much as they hated us when we lost, they loved us even more when we won.

For just the third time since 1960—when I was listening to my hero Tommy McDonald catch a touchdown pass against the Green Bay Packers—the Eagles were going to the playoffs. And this time I wouldn't have to listen on the radio or watch on TV or buy a ticket.

I'd be leading the team onto the field, living out my dream.

EPILOGUE

JUST TWO seasons later, in 1980, Vermeil did what had once seemed impossible: He led the Eagles to the Super Bowl. The team won eleven of its first twelve games; Jaws threw for more than 3,500 yards, added twenty-seven touchdowns, and was named the National Football Conference Player of the Year. Every move Vermeil made seemed prescient as the team beat all the rivals it had been playing bridesmaid to for so long. In the NFC Championship game against the Cowboys, in a frigid Veterans Stadium, the Eagles won 20–7.

While the Eagles lost the Super Bowl to the Oakland Raiders, Vermeil became a Philly hero. Twenty-five years later, his face would still be on billboards near the new Eagles' stadium because companies were sure, more than a generation later, there was still no one more revered than him. Jaws, too, became a civic icon, and settled in the community.

Years later, Vermeil would say that I was one of the main reasons that the team made the Super Bowl. He said my spirit and attitude was the personality infusion the struggling franchise needed when he first became coach, and that my enthusiasm helped lay the foundation for a championship club. Unfortunately, I was no longer on the team when it made its title run.

During the 1979 preseason I suffered a third-degree shoulder separation. It was on a play that became emblematic of my career: a punt coverage takedown. This one was against the Colts in Baltimore. I had played a good game as a receiver and Vermeil took me out, telling me he had seen enough and that I had done well. I had had off-season surgery and my shoulder was throbbing. But, like the season before, the competition at receiver was only getting tougher. I wanted to prove I was so valuable as a special teamer that Vermeil had no choice but to keep me. I begged him to let me go in for one more play. Unfortunately for me, he said yes. I came downfield to make the hit leading with my healthy arm, but the punt returner made a move, forcing me to adjust, and as I drove into him I dislocated my good shoulder. That was it. I couldn't lift my arm.

I wasn't cut right away—NFL teams can't cut you if you're injured while playing—but instead I was put on injured reserve, which turned out to be worse. I lingered around the locker room but was not a part of the team. No one wants to hang with the guy who's hurt. It's as if someone healthy may catch an injury just by standing too close. I was still getting paid, but I couldn't practice with the team. I rehabbed hard for more than two months, and when I finally felt strong enough I begged the trainer to tell Vermeil I was ready, to let me on the field and contribute. But by then I had been passed by. When I was healthy, instead of getting on the roster, I was given my release.

Of course, more than feeling bitter, I felt afraid. No other team was going to pick up a thirty-three-year-old special teamer with one career catch. Especially not one who had missed most of the season with a bum shoulder. Being released the year before was heartbreaking, but this made me sick to my stomach. Going back to television was no longer an option for me—those jobs had been filled when I went back to the Eagles in 1978. I was unemployed and had just built a house and I had no idea how I was going to pay for it. But money was the least of my concerns. For three years I had been riding a wave of popularity that granted me access to a life I had never imagined: luncheons in the city's finest hotels, invitations to speak all over the state, parties full of beautiful people. All of these things had come because of football, because of my journey from the sandlots to the NFL. How many people could say they had been profiled in *Sports Illustrated* or been on *The Mike Douglas Show*? How many people were stopped in the street by total strangers who said they were huge fans? One night when we were in Atlanta during the 1978 season I was hanging out at a bar. A guy came up to me and said, "Hey I recognize you. You're that Rocky guy who plays for the Eagles. I admire what you've done."

But, without the team, I was just a guy who used to play. I didn't have stories from the inside because I was no longer there. And that wasn't just my perspective; that was the truth. Almost immediately I stopped getting calls to hand out awards at Pee Wee football banquets or make speeches to local rotary clubs. After many games we'd won, my house had been where the parties were held. Now my former teammates didn't bother to let me know where they'd be celebrating their wins, which were more and more common. I had a chip on my shoulder. I was way down and had a hard time pulling myself out of it. What I was going through was no different from what any athlete experiences when who he is is tied up in what he does. Being an Eagle—the underdog who fulfilled a dream to play for his favorite team—had become my identity. Without that, I was lost.

That made things difficult at home, too. Sandy knew life with me only as the girlfriend and wife of one of Philly's most popular athletes. Everything was handed to us. We had never been challenged. And when I struggled to figure out what to do with the rest of my life, our marriage struggled. After several years of growing apart, we divorced in 1983.

The next decade was a blur. I tried marketing for Gold's Gyms around Philly and New Jersey. I spent time working in promotions for the Philadelphia Stars, the city's United States

Football League franchise. The team president, Carl Peterson, put me in the radio booth, too. For three years I called games, and being back in football helped my confidence.

Then, in 1990, I did a speaking engagement for the sales-people of U.S. Healthcare. Afterward I was offered a job representing the company at corporate events, making speeches, and, because of my experience in sports, I made some extra money as a personal trainer to the company's top executives. I called this my recovery period: I was working out constantly and getting healthy, both mentally and physically.

After a couple of years at U.S. Healthcare, I was asked by a friend to be on the board of a chain of new day-care centers opening in the area. My friend had asked me to give a presentation to the new board about obesity in children. At the meeting, I put up some charts and graphs. I talked about the poor health of kids, about how much childhood obesity costs parents in healthcare and how a program like the one being provided by the day-care center could help since schools were cutting back on physical education classes.

There was a woman sitting at the boardroom table whom I had never met before. Her name was Janet Cantwell. She was blond, petite, and athletic-looking. When I walked into the room she had caught my eye. This was in July of 1992. By the time I had gotten the courage to call her, she was in Barcelona attending the Summer Olympics.

At our next gathering, in September, 1992, I sought Janet out and asked her to have drinks with me. She accepted.

Janet had been a member of the U.S. Women's Gymnastics team from 1970 to 1973. She then went on to be the gymnastics coach at Penn for twelve years, from 1976 to 1988. She was strong, independent, and impossible to ignore. It didn't take me long to fall in love with her. By the end of 1992 we were living together and I had proposed. We were married August 14, 1993. Nearly five months later, on December 31, 1993, our daughter, Gabriella, was born. Almost three years later, on October 17, 1996, we had a son, Vincent.

Life was as good for me as it had been when I played for the Eagles. Actually, it was sweeter. I had been given a beautiful family at a point in my life when I never expected to have one. Janet, who had been working in real estate for several years, was thriving. I was now working in marketing for Sallie Mae, the student loan company. I didn't need anything else in my life.

But, in the fall of 2002, I got a call from Pete DeStefano, a producer with NFL Films. Before every Monday Night Football game that season they were airing "Distant Replay" segments of former players, and they wanted to do one with me for an Eagles-49ers game coming up at the end of November. It was to honor the twenty-fifth anniversary of *Rocky*. They interviewed me, Denny Franks, Jim Murray, and Ron Jaworski. And it was great to remember how much fun we all had. The piece had old footage of me running through the streets of Philly in the 1970s. They were spliced together with shots from *Rocky* of Sylvester Stallone running up the steps of the art museum. Vermeil talked about how I represented the city, how fans could envision me punching sides of beef the same way Rocky had. There was film of me going crazy on the sidelines, of me wearing my WHO'S NUTS? T-shirt and of my hits on Jimmy Robinson of the Giants and Tony Green of the Redskins. The bitterness of how the Eagles had retired me had faded. And I loved that my kids got to see it.

The next morning my phone was ringing off the hook. Hollywood was calling and several producers wanted to make a movie about my life. For six months Janet and I listened to pitches and promises, not sure who to go with, not sure who could deliver or even what we were looking for. We finally settled on Ken Mok and Victor Constantino of 10 by 10 Entertainment. At first they shopped the NFL Films tape to several studios, but no one was interested without a script. Over the next year, a young screenwriter named Brad Gann and I spent hours on the phone, recapping the most important moments of my life. Finally, in October 2004, the script was auctioned off. Mark Ciardi and Gordon Gray, who had produced *The Rookie* and *Miracle* with Disney, pitched it to Brad Epstein, an exec at the studio. He loved it.

But the movie, *Invincible*, didn't become a reality to me and Janet until the spring of 2005, when Mark Wahlberg decided to take the starring role. I loved the fact that he was doing it. He seemed like he had already lived my story. He was a poor kid from nowhere who had beaten the odds to make something of himself. Before the movie began shooting in July, Mark and Janet and I got together for dinner in New York City. Now that he was on board, I wanted him to understand where I had come from, the path I had taken, and who had influenced me along the way.

Before the drive to New York I had put together a scrapbook. It had pictures of my dad on the pig farm and of my mom playing baseball. There were stories about my days with the Eagles, from when I made the team to the day I was cut. Everything he wanted to know, and probably more, about what made me who I am. As I handed it to him I said, "I'd like you to meet your family. Have as much fun as I have."